Family Child Care

Money Management & Retirement Guide

Being a Family Child Care Professional

Family child care is a special profession for those who love young children. As a professional family child care provider, you must balance the skills required to care for children with those required to operate your business. Here are some tips to help you do this:

- Learn the child care regulations for your area, and follow them.
- Join your local family child care association.
- Sign up with your local child care resource and referral agency.
- Join the Child and Adult Care Food Program (CACFP).
- Find good professional advisors (such as a tax preparer, insurance agent, lawyer).
- Actively participate in training to acquire and improve your professional skills.

Additional Resources

Redleaf Press and Resources for Child Caring are two leading organizations that share the goal of helping your family child care business succeed. Resources for Child Caring (www .resourcesforchildcare.org) can answer your business questions; its Web site is filled with free handouts, articles, and newsletters. Redleaf Press (www.redleafpress.org; 800-423-8309) publishes resources for family child care. We offer the following publications to support your business. For more information, see www.redleafpress.org.

- Starting a family child care business:
  Family Child Care Business Planning Guide

- Promoting your business:
  Family Child Care Marketing Guide

- Creating contracts and policies:
  Family Child Care Contracts and Policies, 3rd Edition
  Redleaf Complete Forms Kit for Family Child Care Providers

- Keeping accurate records and filing your taxes:
  Family Child Care Record-Keeping Guide, 7th Edition
  The Redleaf Calendar-Keeper: A Record-Keeping System for Family Child Care Providers
  C-K Kids: The Online Business Software for Family Child Care Providers
  Family Child Care Tax Workbook and Organizer
  Family Child Care Tax Companion

- Reducing business risks:
  Family Child Care Legal and Insurance Guide

- Managing your money and planning for retirement:
  Family Child Care Money Management and Retirement Guide

(All publications are by Tom Copeland.)

Family Child Care

Money Management & Retirement Guide

Tom Copeland, JD

Redleaf Press®
www.redleafpress.org
800-423-8309

Published by Redleaf Press

10 Yorkton Court

St. Paul, MN 55117

www.redleafpress.org

Printed in the United States of America

16 15 14 13 12 11 10 09   1 2 3 4 5 6 7 8

FSC
Mixed Sources
Product group from well-managed
forests and other controlled sources

Cert no. SW-COC-002283
www.fsc.org
© 1996 Forest Stewardship Council

Library of Congress Cataloging-in-Publication Data

Copeland, Tom.

  Family child care money management & retirement guide / Tom Copeland.

    p. cm.

  Includes index.

  ISBN 978-1-60554-009-2

  1. Family day care—United States—Management. 2. Family day care—Economic aspects—United States. 3. Family day care—United States—Finance. 4. Retirement—Planning. I. Title.

  HQ778.63.C664 2008

  362.71'2—dc22

                    2008032783

Disclaimer

Redleaf Press and the author are not engaged in rendering legal, accounting, or financial advice or any other professional services, and we are not responsible for the outcome of how the information in this book is interpreted or applied. Readers who want professional advice about their money or investments should consult a qualified, experienced financial advisor. Although this book uses certain mutual funds and investments as examples, we are not recommending that readers buy any specific fund or investment. We also aren't advising readers to hire a financial advisor, even though we discuss the circumstances in which professional advice might be helpful.

Printed on acid-free paper

Contents

Part II: Understand Your Options

Part III: Prepare for Retirement

Appendix

Preface

My mother and father, Carol and Bruce Copeland, have been my inspiration for this book. When my three sisters and I were very little, they taught us to put our quarters into a piggy bank. When I was about ten, they helped me open a savings account at our local bank. I remember getting a free Kodak Instamatic camera for opening the account. (The plastic camera later melted when I left it in the back seat of the car.) Later my parents decided to give us more responsibility in managing our money by increasing our allowances and making us pay for most of the things that we needed.

When I was about twelve, one of my teachers assigned a class project in which each student got $500 in fake money to invest wherever he or she wanted; after one month we would see who had earned the most money. I "invested" as much as I could in my father's company, Connecticut General Life Insurance, and put the little that was left into IBM stock. I tracked the progress of my stocks on graph paper and watched as the tracking line went straight up each week. I won the competition hands-down. (The boy who came in second sat behind me and had also "bought" IBM at my recommendation.) As a prize for winning the contest, I got to meet with a local stockbroker.

Those early experiences have stayed with me my entire life. As I grew older, I asked my father countless questions about managing money and planning for retirement—and I still highly value his advice. Throughout his working life, my father has held a range of jobs, including life insurance salesman, president of a life insurance company, Realtor, and financial planner. He has always believed that people's faith should be lived out in their daily work, and that the way we handle our money should align with our values. He has put this belief into action by using his financial skills to support organizations that are working to create a more just world.

My mother taught me the values of persistence, appreciation for what you have, and unpretentiousness. She is creative and artistic—but also detail-oriented, well-organized, and very conservative about money. Many of my mother's qualities have inspired me as I manage my own money. Both my parents have been wonderful role models for me, and they are responsible for much of my success in life.

Acknowledgments

Many people have contributed to this book, including thousands of family child care providers who have shared their stories in my training sessions over the past 26 years and over 500 providers who responded to the online money management survey discussed in this book. Thanks to all of them.

Thanks also to the following people, who reviewed this book and offered valuable suggestions that made it better:

- Tax and financial planning professionals: Benjamin Cohen, Barbara Delbene, Tom Jemison, Shaun McHale, Jeff Robinson, Sandy Schroeder, Al Wroblewski, and Pinghau Yin.

- Family child care providers: Olga Anderson, Sarah Beck, Kalissa Braga, Laurie De Martini, Pat Goor, Traci Heilman, Roxanne Johnson, Patty Kelly, Bonna Lake, Patricia Lee, Debbie Moore, Linda Powell, Tiffany Sartin, Pamela Schmitz, Loretta Spindler, Lorna Tall, Michelle Thole, and Reva Wywadis.

Others who have contributed to this book include Jan Stokley, Diane Copeland, Kathy Modigliani, and Paul Bloomer. Thanks to Ann Forstie for the section on free credit reports in chapter 3. Thanks to David Heath for project management; Laurie Herrmann, Carla Valadez, Douglas Schmitz, and Jim Handrigan for production assistance; and Jan Grover and Beth Wright for proofreading.

I want to give special thanks to my editor, Rose Brandt. Rose has been my editor for six previous books, and her work has greatly contributed to their success. She is a painstakingly thorough editor who has improved the clarity of all my books. Her work on this book is especially noteworthy, and her numerous suggestions have improved every section.
I cannot thank her enough for many years of excellent work.

How This Book Can Help You

This book will help you learn to manage your money better. It will describe workable strategies that you can use to reduce your expenses, make more money, and get out of debt. It will educate you about the unique financial issues that family child care providers face in scenarios such as buying a car or van, hiring an employee, or closing your business. It will explain how to figure out how much you should be saving for retirement and how to invest your retirement savings. Taken together, these strategies will improve your ability to operate a successful business and build the foundation for a solid financial future.

I wrote this book to help you worry less about money, leaving you with more time for the things you enjoy most—caring for children and spending time with your family.

Money Management in Family Child Care

A family child care provider is a person who loves children and has taken the initiative to start up her own business and become her own boss. However, caring for children and running a business are very different activities that require different skills.

As a family child care provider, you most likely entered the field with some experience raising your own children, and you're probably very comfortable helping children learn. You may even have taken training in child development to improve your child care skills. However, if you're like most providers, you've had no training (and comparatively little experience) in managing business finances. As a result, you may feel unsure when faced with the multitude of financial decisions that are involved in running a family child care business.

Because of this lack of training, family child care providers worry a lot about their finances. I know this because in 2007 we posted a money management survey on our Web site. (You can view the results of this survey at www.redleafpress.org. Type "money management" in the search box and follow the links.) We got responses from over 500 family child care providers across the country—and found that many of you are concerned with how to get out of debt, maintain your financial health, and prepare for retirement. Here's how some of you described your biggest financial worry:

My biggest financial worry is how to pay for my monthly bills. Saving for retirement just isn't possible. Day care is so unpredictable—whenever I begin to get on my feet financially, a client moves away, and my husband and I have to live on credit cards to make ends meet for a while. It's scary.

My biggest worry is that I'll have a major injury or illness that will prevent me from running my business. I fear that I'll run out of time before my financial goals are met.

I worry that we won't have enough money for retirement, and I will have to work forever.

Paying off my debt while I'm still able to work is a serious worry. With each passing year I realize that this is an exceptionally physically demanding job, and I wonder how many more years I can handle it.

My biggest financial worry is that I won't be able to meet my house payment for the current month.

My biggest worry is that when I retire I won't have any financial support because I didn't save while I was working.

My biggest financial worry is getting my credit cards paid down so that I can start putting away money for retirement.

Since this wasn't a scientific survey, we know that the responses we got aren't statistically representative of all the family child care providers in the United States—however, the 517 providers who took our survey did span a wide geographic and demographic range:

- They hailed from across the country, from California to Virginia, and Minnesota to Texas.

- Their average age was 41 years old—the youngest was 21, and the oldest was 67.

- They had been in business for an average of 10 years—ranging from "just starting out" to 40 years of experience. (As a group, our survey respondents were more experienced than the average for all family child care providers.)

- They expected to continue working in family child care for another 11 years, on average.

When asked how comfortable they were with their current financial situation, 13% of our respondents said they were "very comfortable," 52% said they were "somewhat comfortable," and 35% said they were "not at all comfortable."

Although almost all of them (92%) described themselves as either "somewhat knowledgeable" (66%) or "very knowledgeable" (26%) about managing their finances, a large percentage were having difficulty putting this knowledge into practice:

- Only 13% had long-term care insurance (to pay their ongoing medical bills in case of a major illness such as a stroke or Alzheimer's disease).

- Only 13% had disability income insurance (to replace some of their income if they became disabled for a long period).

- Only 18% were prepared to make a down payment of at least 75% of the cost of their next car.

- Only 23% had prepared an annual budget for their business in the previous year.

- Only 27% had three months of living expenses saved in an emergency fund.

- Only 39% were paying their credit card bill in full each month. The average unpaid credit card balance was $5,084.

To get some perspective on these numbers, these family child care providers are far from alone in their financial predicament. Most Americans, regardless of their income, are uneasy about their money and unprepared for retirement. In general, family child care providers are similar to other Americans—for example, the national median credit card balance is $2,200; in our survey, the median (not average) credit card balance was $2,000.

I normally do workshops for family child care providers—but if I were asked to do a financial planning workshop for a group of lawyers and doctors, I'd have to cover many of the same issues that I usually do, and I'd expect them to have financial problems similar to those of family child care providers, although perhaps on a bigger scale.

Still, it's true that one of the reasons why providers aren't more financially secure is that it's difficult to get rich caring for children. In our survey, 74% of the respondents reported a business profit (business income less business expenses) of less than $20,000 in the previous year, and only 27 of them (5%) had made a profit of $40,000 or more. Although low earnings are one reason why many family child care providers find it difficult to save money and manage their finances, it's far from the only one. The responses to our survey listed several other common obstacles to saving money:

I've got two children in college, and I'm paying a lot for health insurance.

I don't know where and how to start managing my money better—I'm pretty inexperienced with handling my own finances.

I'm raising an infant granddaughter.

We're just not dedicated enough to saving. There is money there, but we manage to spend it all before we can save it.

I keep putting it off.

The day care business in my area is very unpredictable.

I save enough money, but I don't know how to make it work for me.

I'm irresponsible with money and always have been.

I think I don't have the discipline because my money issues aren't really about money, they're about power—and I think I'm a bit scared of having more power over my life.

Two of the respondents described quite vividly the difficult circumstances that many family child care providers face in their struggle to get ahead financially:

My husband and I run our child care business together—this is our only job and source of income. We both worry about retiring some day. We're in our mid-forties now, and we feel as if every year it's getting harder and harder to take care of 12 children for the long hours that we work—but we feel unable to make a change, because neither of us can get a job making the kind of money that we make now. Still, we can't get ahead because we have high expenses—we're putting our daughter through college, and our younger son is still at home. We'd love to know that some day we'll be able to sit back and rest and be financially secure.

Although I believe that family child care is the ideal way to care for and educate young children, I'm having trouble seeing how, with the current state of the field in our culture, I can possibly make a go of it in a financially healthy way. I'm stumped.

However, not all providers are struggling financially; in fact, some are doing quite well:

We save 100% of one income, plus more whenever we can. Our home is three years old and already paid for—we have enough money to cover all our needs, and we have NO debt!

We have been able to save up enough money to purchase two rental houses that will generate income when we are retired.

My husband and I have been using all our extra money to pay off our debt, and we're almost done. Then we'll be able to add that extra money to our retirement savings.

My husband has a great retirement plan.

We're currently paying off our debt and building a three-month emergency fund; the retirement fund comes next.

First Steps Toward Financial Health

Although the kinds of financial challenges described in the responses to our survey may appear overwhelming, those issues aren't insurmountable. You may find it a lot easier to care for children than to take charge of your finances—but you *can* learn those new skills.

How do I know this? By starting your own business, you have shown that you are an entrepreneur—you're willing to take risks and aren't afraid of a challenge. In fact, if you think about what you have accomplished so far, you may find that you have already come a long way in meeting your original financial goals.

Still, if you're reading this book, you probably aren't wealthy yet. Many family child care providers struggle to make ends meet, and you may be worried that you won't ever have enough money to retire. You may also feel that you lack the knowledge needed to manage your finances more effectively. Although some providers are comfortable making their own long-term investment decisions, many others don't yet understand the basics of saving and investing.

This book will help you gain more financial control over your life and business, whether the level of your current financial knowledge is novice, expert, or something in between. Here's how it can help you:

- Part I explains how to learn new spending habits, increase your savings, get out of debt, earn more money, and prioritize your financial goals.

- Part II guides you through some decisions that can have major financial consequences, including buying a car, applying for a grant or loan, hiring employees, moving your business outside of your home, and handling the financial aspects of getting a divorce or closing your business.

- Part III covers the basics of retirement planning, including maximizing your Social Security benefits, figuring out how much you should be saving for retirement, choosing your retirement investments and IRAs, and working with a financial advisor.

Although the primary focus of this book is improving your financial well-being, I understand that money isn't the most important thing in your life. In fact, the financial rewards of your work may be less important than being able to share your love with the children and watch them grow every day. As one provider told me, "I love being a family child care provider. It's less a job, and more a way of life."

Ultimately, there's no contradiction between providing high-quality child care and being financially successful. I hope that you recognize this, and that this book will strengthen your ability to meet both your personal and your financial goals.

• •

A Note about Gender

Studies show that over 95% of family child care providers are female. In this book I will use female pronouns to describe family child care providers and male pronouns to describe their spouses. I've made this choice to avoid the awkward use of "she or he"; however, I don't mean to slight any male family child care providers or female spouses who may be reading this book.

• •

What This Book Doesn't Cover

This book doesn't address every issue related to managing money and retirement planning. For example, it doesn't cover the financial issues related to insurance, such as long-term care insurance, disability income insurance, and health insurance. For information about these topics, see the *Family Child Care Legal and Insurance Guide.*

This book also doesn't cover estate planning (how your assets will be divided after you die), writing a will, supporting elderly parents, or saving money for college. It also doesn't discuss the importance of assigning a medical power of attorney. (This is a legal document that gives another person the authority to make medical decisions on your behalf if you become unable to do so.)

This book only attempts to cover the basic concepts of retirement planning and investing. It doesn't delve into more complex topics, such as investing in limited partnerships, trusts, or precious metals, or how to draw down your money in retirement.

In addition, the discussion of retirement planning in this book is based on the assumption that most readers are novice investors who aren't interested in becoming experts. Fortunately, as we'll see, you don't need to become an expert investor to make wise, informed decisions about your money and attain your retirement goals.

• •

The Tax Laws May Change

This book was written in 2008. Since the tax laws can change rapidly, the discussion of taxes in this book may be outdated by the time you read it. For the latest information about tax laws, consult a tax professional or the *Family Child Care Tax Workbook and Organizer* for the tax year in question.

• •

PART I

Manage Your Money

CHAPTER ONE

Reduce Your Spending

Chapter Summary
This chapter focuses on helping you learn the fundamental financial skill of controlling your spending. It starts by showing you how to track your spending and identify where you might cut back on your expenses. It discusses how to develop new spending habits and provides a range of strategies for doing so.

This chapter begins a discussion of personal money management that will continue through chapter 5. The goal of this first part of the book is to help you gain more control over your money and learn to make healthier financial decisions.

Many people feel anxious and out of control when it comes to their finances—money is the cause of a great deal of the stress in our lives. In fact, many people can't even bear to face their financial problems since their feelings of shame, fear, and stress make those problems seem insurmountable. If that sounds familiar, the solution lies in learning better money management skills that will inspire you to face your situation head-on and start making real changes. The purpose of this book is to help you do that.

Since managing your money begins with reducing your expenses, in this chapter I'll focus on explaining how you can start getting your spending under control. You may wonder why I'm starting there, rather than showing you how to increase your income right away. (As you'll see later, I do have lots of suggestions about how you can earn more money.)

I could start by showing you how to increase your income if your financial problems could be magically solved by earning a little more money. However, if your expenses aren't under control at this point, adding more money won't help; it will simply increase the size of your problem. (If you don't believe me, consider how many millionaires have gone bankrupt—lots!) If you're struggling financially, learning to control your expenses will be the first step in developing a healthier relationship with your money.

Track Your Spending Exercise

If you're like most people, you've thought a lot about how you might earn more money. You might also have said to yourself, "Gee, I really *should* reduce my expenses." However, have you considered what it would really take to spend less? Learning to control your spending is the first and most fundamental financial skill—if you lack this ability, nothing else you do will help very much (like all those millionaires who went bankrupt).

To start learning how to control your spending, you need to know where your money is going. Here's an exercise that will help you figure that out. (If you already know exactly where your money is going every month, congratulations! Few people do. However, I'd suggest that you complete this exercise anyway—you may learn something new.) After explaining how to do the exercise, I'll describe how to use your results to understand your spending habits better.

This exercise starts with tracking your family's spending for at least one month—and ideally for two or three months. Proceed as follows:

1. During the month, write down the amount of every item your family spends money on, including a description of each expense so you'll remember what it was for.

2. At the end of the month, go over the expenses you recorded and divide them into two categories, fixed expenses and flexible expenses:

   • **Fixed expenses** are expenses that you have little or no control over (like your mortgage)—you *must* spend that amount of money this month.

   • **Flexible expenses** are expenses over which you have at least some control (like your food bill)—you *could* spend less, if you could figure out how to do it.

3. Go through the expenses in each category and lump them into logical subtotals, such as food, clothing, insurance, utilities, and so on. (The specific categories don't matter, as long as they make sense to you.)

4. Create a two-column table to add up your fixed and flexible expenses for the month. Under each column, list the subtotals. (If you do this exercise for more than one month, create a table for each month.)

Table 1 shows an example of what your first monthly spending table might look like. Of course, your expenses might be very different from the numbers used in this example, so the subtotals shown here may not be the best categories for you to use. It will be most helpful to use subtotals that reflect your own spending patterns. For example, if you're consistently spending money on books, CDs, toys, take-out coffee, or household supplies, then you should show a subtotal for that expense category. (It's especially important to customize your subtotals like this for your flexible expenses.)

If you're having trouble deciding whether an expense is fixed or flexible, lean toward putting it in the flexible column. Resist the temptation to put an expense in the fixed column unless you really didn't have a choice about spending that money this month. For example,

Table 1. Example spending table

Our spending for January

Fixed expenses		Flexible expenses	
Mortgage (or rent)	$600	Food	$500
Property tax	$300	Clothing	$200
Gas	$100	Gas	$150
Insurance (personal and business)	$1,000	Vacation	$200
Car loan	$350	Entertainment	$100
Credit card payment	$550	Cable television	$50
Utilities (gas, electric, water, phone)	$200	Charitable contribution	$150
Student loan	$400	Hobbies	$100
		Child care supplies	$100
		Other business expenses	$200
Total fixed expenses	$3,500	*Total flexible expenses*	$1,750

you could put some of your gas expenses under the fixed column, since you have to buy a certain amount of gas each month. However, don't list everything you spent on gas this month in that column, because some of that spending was probably flexible.

If you do this exercise for just a month or two, you won't account for all your expenses, since some large expenses occur infrequently—fixed expenses such as homeowners insurance, car insurance, and property taxes; and flexible expenses such as furniture, computer hardware and software, and seasonal and holiday expenses. If you want to try to include all your infrequent expenses in your table, you could add them up into two annual totals (fixed and flexible), divide the totals by 12 to get the average cost per month, and add these sub-totals to your monthly table.

If you don't have good records of your spending for the last 12 months, then just do your best to estimate these totals, and refine your estimates over time as you track your actual spending.

Review Your Table

Once your first monthly table is done, use it to improve your understanding of your financial habits and circumstances. Ask yourself the following questions:

- **Is my spending level sustainable?** Compare the total of your fixed and flexible expenses to your total income for the month. If your expenses were higher than your income, this is a clear sign that your finances need immediate attention—you won't be able to sustain this level of spending without going deeper and deeper into debt. This book will give you the tools you need to make real changes so that you can start creating a healthier financial future for yourself.

- **What does my spending say about my values?** You work hard for your money, and the way you spend it is an indication of your values. Ask yourself what your spending this month says about what you value most. For example, if you're in debt, are spending thousands of dollars on clothes every year, and haven't saved much for retirement, this shows that you place a high value on current consumption and a low value on providing a comfortable future for yourself.

Take time to consider how you're spending your money. If your spending behavior doesn't match your true priorities in life, you may want to become more purposeful about how you're using your resources. This can be a powerful motivation for changing your habits.

The Culture of Spending

Unlike in our great-grandparents' generation, spending money now rather than saving for tomorrow has become a fact of life for many people. This habit has been greatly encouraged—if not created—by the culture of spending that has grown up around us. Every day we're bombarded with advertising messages that urge us to spend, spend, spend. All our media—television, radio, newspapers, magazines, billboards, and the Internet—are constantly urging us to spend more. We've even become walking billboards ourselves, since it's become fashionable to wear clothes that prominently feature the maker's name.

We've been trained to accept our role as consumers without question, and most of us own far too many things that we haven't yet paid for. As a result, most people in our culture place a higher value on spending for today than on meeting their long-term financial needs, such as preparing for their children's college education or a comfortable retirement. They don't acknowledge the fact that not being able to provide for their family's future needs is a sign that they're living beyond their means.

When was the last time you heard an advertisement say, "Hey, you! Thinking about spending money? Stop! Don't do it! Save your money instead! This message brought to you by . . . " Wait a minute—who would sponsor such an advertisement? Even your bank can make more money by selling you other financial products than by encouraging you to save. So you'll never hear such an ad because no business can make much money by selling the idea of saving rather than spending.

To change our financial habits, we need to start noticing and questioning all the messages that are urging us to spend. We also need to counter their influence by developing our own internal messages and motivations for saving money instead of spending it.

Don't Show Your Love by Spending

It's natural to love the children in your program and want to show your love in every way you can. The only problem with this natural desire is that too many providers make the mistake of thinking that expressing their love means spending more money on the children. But showing your love *doesn't* mean spending more.

Some providers keep buying more or larger toys every year until their closets, basement, and garage are all overflowing. One provider, Pat from Minnesota, told me that many providers have turned their habit of buying children's items that they don't really need into a "hobby." Certainly, toys are an important part of helping children learn. However, providing a hundred toys won't help children learn that much more than far fewer toys, and it may even be counterproductive.

• •

Are You Spending to Meet Emotional Needs?

Some providers tend to spend money to meet their emotional needs—to express their love, improve their mood, get approval from others, outdo other providers, and so on. If this is your pattern, you're probably aware of how easily it can lead to overspending. Learn to notice when you feel the urge to spend for an emotional reason, and look for another way to meet that need instead.

I'm not saying that you should never buy flowers to brighten up your day, but I do believe that it's healthier to learn how to meet your emotional needs in ways that don't involve spending money.

Once you let go of your emotional reasons for spending money, you can focus on more rational reasons, such as replacing a broken toy, meeting an educational objective, or satisfying a physical need (such as food, housing, or clothing).

• •

The parents of most of the children in your care won't expect you to spend a lot of money on their children. In fact, if you do, they may feel uncomfortable and worry that they won't be able to keep up with you. (If you're not sure about the parents' attitudes, ask them.) The providers who responded to our survey agreed that you don't need to spend a lot to provide a quality environment for the children:

Learn to set a budget, and don't let your heart take over and buy too many things just because you love the kids. You have to set limits on holidays and birthdays. It's really important to put the cash away for emergencies before you get into a situation where you have no extra money to spare.

Stop making so many purchases for your business. You really don't need another book or toy. Use the resources you have. You don't need one of each kind of whatever it is you want.

Stop spending money on your business—it's too easy to "nickel and dime" away your cash for new things that you don't really need. I have updated my equipment and environment with quality items—but it's the little stuff that really adds up without adding much to my business.

Stop buying so much stuff for your day care. Most providers I know continually buy junk because it's on sale or a good deal at a garage sale. Then they have too much stuff, and complain that they can't get organized.

Save, save, and spend only what you need to. Reduce, repurpose, reuse, trade. You do have to be creative, but kids don't need expensive toys to be happy and keep learning.

You can always find ways to save a few dollars here and there. Your day care children don't need the best of everything to stay happy and be well taken care of.

As Heidi from Wisconsin says, "I've watched other providers spend too much, and I don't want to be like that. I've tried to warn other providers, 'If you start out caring for two or three children, and then expand your program to five or six, don't spend more money. Live within your means.'"

Small Amounts Add Up Quickly

Some providers buy small items for the children whenever they go shopping—candy, small toys, or other treats. Others tend to spend a little bit every day on small discretionary expenses, such as bottled water or takeout coffee. You may be thinking that these little purchases couldn't make much difference—"It's only $10, so why not buy it?" However, this attitude is usually a sign that you're in denial about spending beyond your means. Although each of these purchases may be small, if you're watching your spending, you'll know that they add up quickly.

Being able to resist the urge to spend even a small amount of money is one of the first signs that you're developing wiser spending habits—and over time this change can make a big difference. Let's take a look at how small decisions about spending or saving can add up:

- If you spend $5 a day on takeout coffee or treats for the children for five days a week, 50 weeks a year, it will add up to an expense of $1,250 a year.

- If you instead invest the same amount ($25 a week) in a tax-deferred investment that earns 8% a year, after 10 years you will end up with $19,127 for your retirement.

The difference between these "small" choices is over $20,000!

Nevertheless, some providers assume that it's fine to spend more as long as they're spending the money on items for their business. They figure that they'll be able to deduct all their expenses on their tax return anyway, so they might as well spend the money rather than give it to the IRS. Is that true? Let's run the numbers and find out:

Let's say that you're in a 40% tax bracket (25% federal income tax plus 15% Social Security tax), and you have $1,000 in your checkbook. You're considering spending $100 on an item for your business. If you buy that item, you'll only reduce your taxes by $40. The net effect is that your $1,000 will be reduced to $940 ($1,000 − $100 + $40 = $940). If you had saved the $100 instead, you would still have the entire $100, plus you'd have started accumulating interest that would gradually build your savings.

The bottom line? Regardless of your tax bracket, it never makes sense to spend money just to reduce your taxes. In this example, the provider spent $100 in order to save just $40 in taxes. That's not a very good bargain.

• •

Spending Less Pays Off

In general, providers who earn a higher business profit accomplish this primarily by spending less rather than by charging higher rates. To see why, consider two providers who are caring for the same number of children and charging the same fees. Although they both start with the same income, the one who keeps her expenses lower will always have a bigger profit, and thus more money to set aside for her short- and long-term financial goals.

• •

Strategies for Reducing Your Expenses

Regardless of your income, having a healthy relationship with money means living within your means—keeping your annual spending below your annual income while putting away enough money for your short- and long-term financial goals.

Many providers who are living beyond their means find that it is easier to reduce their expenses than to increase their income. Even providers who earn very little can usually find ways to reduce their expenses by a small amount here and there—and, as we've just seen, those small amounts can add up quickly.

Here are some strategies that other providers have successfully used to reduce their expenses:

- Linda from California asks parents to bring her business supplies from a list that she keeps posted in her home. The list includes items such as scratch paper, card stock, markers, and crayons. At Christmas, she gives parents a wish list of items she can use for her business. (Before that, they were giving her Christmas gifts that she couldn't use, such as bubble bath and perfumed powder.)

- Tiffany from Illinois helps pay for her monthly birthday parties by posting a list of items that she needs parents to bring, such as food, juice, pizza, games, or a veggie tray. For her last Halloween party, the parents brought everything she needed, so the party didn't cost her anything.

- Olga from California says that she keeps her expenses low by being well organized. She keeps careful track of her supplies and materials so that she can avoid buying something she already owns just because she can't find it.

- Roxanne from North Dakota charges parents an annual supply fee of $75. This fee covers her expenses for broken toys, damage to her home, and carpet cleaning, plus supplies such as her hand soap dispenser, paper towels, dish soap, toilet paper, pencils, coloring books, birthday posters, and costumes for the children. She has also saved $500 a year by stopping her practice of giving a treat to the children every Friday.

- Before she buys something, Pat from Minnesota asks herself, "Will this improve my business, will it entice parents to come to my program, or will it not matter?" "Mostly it doesn't matter," she says, and that realization helps her avoid spending money on things that she doesn't need.

Here are some additional suggestions from other providers that you may wish to try in your program:

Have parents bring a food item that you can use to prepare a main dish for lunch with the children. Then make enough of that dish so that you can give the remainder to the parents for their family dinner.

I can't afford to transport children in my car any more because of the high cost of car insurance. So now I take the children on field trips on the city bus and charge their parents for the bus fare.

I suggest that you go to household auctions, where you can often buy arts and craft supplies, games, puzzles, and toys for pennies on the dollar. One year I was able to get all my Christmas decorations for just $10!

• •

Deposit the Money You Receive Promptly

Unlike an employee who gets a paycheck every two weeks—and may never even see the money if it's directly deposited into her checking account—most family child care providers are in regular contact with money. You may be paid on a weekly basis, or even more often, if your clients don't all pay on the same day. So you may be receiving payments several times a week, and often they're in cash.

This constant flow of money may tempt you into thinking that you have a lot of money to spend, but of course, this isn't true. In fact, your profit may be only a small portion of what you earn.

To overcome the temptation to spend your money right away, put all the money you receive right into your checking account—especially the cash! This habit will help you resist the urge to spend money that you need to cover your expenses.

• •

Rethink Your Habits

Finding ways to save money may mean rethinking some old habits, but just because you've done something the same way for years, that doesn't mean you can't change it.

- Stop buying children's toys and supplies at the retail price; instead, start going to Goodwill, consignment shops, and yard sales.

- Start using the library for children's books and videos rather than buying them.

- Start using dishrags instead of paper towels.

- Stop buying small garbage bags; reuse your grocery bags instead.

- Cut back on eating out and groceries. Eat less meat. Stop buying bottled water.

- Stop smoking.

- Cut back on buying lottery tickets and takeout coffee.

- If you're regularly paying ATM fees or late fees at the video store or library, change your habits to avoid these charges.

- If your bank is still sending you your cancelled checks each month, cancel this service—banks now charge extra for it.

Look online for more suggestions for living frugally—there are many Web sites devoted to living on less, including www.thefrugalshopper.com, www.simpleliving.net, and www.frugaliving.com. To find more resources, do an Internet search for "living cheaply," "frugal living," or "voluntary simplicity."

Little Steps Count

Here are some small steps that can add up:

- Ask other providers for any toys that they are no longer using.

- Ask parents to donate any children's items that they no longer need—toys, equipment, supplies, and so on.

- When you hear that another local provider is going out of business, call her and see if she'd be willing to donate her toys and supplies to you—and if not, whether you could buy them at a discount.

- Put all your change away in a savings jar.

- Buy items in bulk whenever possible—toilet paper, cleaning supplies, light bulbs, laundry detergent, etc.

- Buy the lowest-octane gas available, and don't drive faster than the speed limit (speeding reduces your gas mileage).

- The next time you raise your rates, don't raise your spending; instead, put the extra income directly into a savings or investment account.

- If you donate your old clothes and toys to a charity, rather than selling them at a garage sale, visit the Web site itsdeductibleonline.intuit.com to determine their current value. Then deduct the total as a noncash charity deduction on **Schedule A**.

Look for Big Steps Too
Consider these potential opportunities to reduce your spending:

- If you get a windfall, don't spend it. Whenever you get an extra lump of money, such as a rebate check or an overpayment refund, save it—don't spend it.

- To reduce your insurance premiums, raise the deductibles on your homeowners and vehicle insurance policies to at least $500, and preferably $1,000. Don't spend the resulting savings; put it directly into a savings account each month.

- The next time you're in the market for a car, get a vehicle that has good gas mileage.

- Contact your energy company to see if it can conduct an energy audit on your home. Increasing the energy efficiency of your home can save you a lot of money. If the audit makes a recommendation that would require a large investment, such as installing new windows, consider how long you'll be living in the home to determine whether the payback will be worth it.

Smart Shopping Tips
Here are some tips that can help reduce your spending while shopping:

- Shop alone.

- Make a list before you go, and don't buy anything that isn't on your list.

- Bring a limited amount of cash, and leave your checkbook and debit card at home.

- Identify the stores where you spend too much. Before you visit one of those stores, set a limit on how much you will spend on that visit.

- Eat before you shop for food or groceries.

- Take a calculator with you to the grocery store and add up every item you place in your cart to make sure you don't exceed your food budget. That way you won't be surprised when you get to the register.

- Don't shop if you're in a bad mood—people often spend more to improve their mood.

CHAPTER TWO

Increase Your Savings

Chapter Summary
This chapter describes ways to save more money, with many suggestions from other providers. It explains the difference between short- and long-term savings and the different kinds of savings accounts that are available for short-term savings. It also explains the best approach to teaching your children to save.

I have found that most providers seem to follow a "savings plan" that involves just getting through the month as best they can, and then seeing if there's any money left over after they pay their bills. The problem with this approach is that there's likely to be too little—or nothing—left over at the end of the month. Instead, the approach I recommend is that you put your savings away at the start of the month, and then reduce your spending on flexible expenses during the month as needed to avoid running out of money.

In the words of a provider who took our survey, "Put away your savings *before* you take out your spending money. Make saving your first priority." Other child care providers agree with her:

Take a set amount, and put it away. Learn to live on as little as possible, so that when you make more, you'll be able to save it and won't need it as income.

Start saving immediately—with your first paycheck.

Save a certain percentage of your income, no matter how little you make in the beginning.

Start saving as soon as you open your business. Each week, take a few dollars from one parent's payment, and save it.

Where to Find the Money

At this point you may be thinking, "Sure, Tom, I'd love to save more—but where am I supposed to find the money on my income?" The answer to saving more isn't increasing your income—although that can be helpful, and we'll look at ways to do that in chapter 4. Just consider that lots of people who make far more than you do aren't saving enough either.

Regardless of how much you earn, finding some money to save will always be fundamentally a matter of making saving a higher priority than some of your discretionary spending. This means that the first—and most important—step in finding more money to save will be looking more closely at your spending patterns, starting with the spending exercise in chapter 1.

For example, let's say that your goal is to save an additional $100 a month. In my experience, most providers who complete the spending exercise in chapter 1 are able to identify some items in their flexible expenses column that they could spend less on. You'll need to look at the spending columns in your table and make your own decisions about what you might reduce based on your own priorities. However, if you really want to save more, you will be able to identify at least some small ways to cut back, even if they don't seem to amount to much.

Don't worry if you can't find the entire $100 right away. Start by looking for small amounts that you can add to your savings—a few dollars here and there. Putting aside even a few dollars a week will help you develop the habit of saving and thinking about your long-term financial needs. It's better to save a little bit on a regular basis and watch it add up than to set an overly ambitious goal and get discouraged because you can't reach it right away.

• •

Is Your Debt Too High?

For many people, the main barrier to saving more money is that they have very high fixed expenses. If your required monthly expenses take up such a large portion of your income that you can't find any ways to cut back, review the fixed expenses column in your spending table, and consider which of these expenses you could cut with the least amount of pain. For many people, the answer will be the interest they are paying on their debt—their credit cards, car loan, college loan, home equity loan, and mortgage. For a discussion of how to balance the goals of saving more and paying off your debt, see chapter 3.

• •

You Can't Save by Spending

When looking for ways to save, don't be confused by the way advertisers have corrupted the word *saving* to mean spending. When shopping, we're bombarded with messages that claim we can save money by buying something that's on sale. But in fact, buying something on sale requires us to *spend* our money, not *save* it.

Saving means putting money aside to use later; it doesn't mean buying something for less. When you buy a $100 item at 20% off, you're actually spending $80, not saving $20. I'm not suggesting that you ignore sales on items that you need anyway. Spending wisely will help you reduce your expenses so that you can add more to your savings. Nevertheless, too often people use a sale as an excuse to spend money on things they don't really need— "Look how much I *saved*!"

When you're tempted to buy something on sale, look at how much you'll be spending, and ask yourself whether you need that item more than you need that money in your savings account. (Bear in mind the $20,000 difference between spending and saving that we saw in the previous chapter.) If you do sometimes slip up and spend some extra money at a sale, get into the habit of putting all the money you "saved" into a real savings account. For example, in the above example, you'd put your $20 "savings" into a savings account.

Short-Term and Long-Term Savings

When setting a target for how much you'd like to save each month, you'll want to consider both your short-term and your long-term financial needs. You'll also need to put these two kinds of savings into different kinds of "savings accounts," since you'll have different financial goals for them.

Short-Term Savings

You put money into **short-term savings** to set it aside for major expenses that are likely to occur in one to five years and that will require more funds than you'll have on hand otherwise. Your short-term savings will include your emergency fund for unexpected expenses, as well as any other savings you might need to buy your next car, make a down payment on a home, do a home improvement, take a nice vacation, or buy a boat.

The goal for your short-term savings is to preserve your money so that it will be there when you need it. Although you may earn some interest on this money, you won't get a very high interest rate, since you can't afford to take any risks with it. Although the value of your deposits may be somewhat eroded by inflation, over this short time frame that won't make much difference. Your short-term savings should also be readily accessible, since you may need to withdraw the money on short notice. The options that will allow you to meet these short-term goals are these:

- savings accounts (at your bank and online)
- money market funds
- certificates of deposit (CDs)
- short-term bond funds

Long-Term Savings

You invest money into **long-term savings** to make sure you'll have enough income to support yourself in retirement and meet other long-term financial goals. Most people, especially self-employed people, won't be able to retire on the income they will get from

Social Security and pensions. Chapters 11 and 12 explain how to figure out how much you'll be getting from Social Security, how much you're likely to need in order to retire, and how much you should be saving now to fill the gap between the two.

The goal for your long-term investments is just the opposite of the goal for your short-term savings. In order to have enough money to retire on, you'll need to invest this money and give it the opportunity to grow faster than inflation, which will require you to take more risks with it. In addition, this long-term money doesn't need to be readily accessible—in fact, the idea is to put it away and never touch it until you retire. The options that will allow you to meet these long-term goals include stocks, bonds, and real estate. Planning and investing for retirement is a very important topic—which I'll cover in depth in Part III—but in this chapter, I'm going to focus on short-term savings.

Where to Put Your Short-Term Savings

Once you have come up with a few dollars to put away for your short-term savings, you'll need to decide where to stash it. We have seen that there are basically four places to put the money that you are likely to need in the next one to five years. So let's take a look at each of these options in more detail.

Savings Accounts

You probably opened your first passbook savings account at your local bank as a kid. Today **savings accounts** at banks and credit unions are much less popular because they pay the lowest interest and more people are aware that they have other options. The biggest advantages of this option are that it's convenient and there's no risk that you'll lose money, since your bank deposits are insured by the government (up to $100,000 per account). You can open a savings account with very little money and withdraw your money at any time without a penalty. Interest is usually compounded monthly or quarterly. Sometimes there will be a monthly service charge, and some savings accounts have additional limitations, such as a minimum balance.

• •

Should You Keep Your Savings in Your Checking Account?
Some banks and credit unions offer checking accounts that will pay you a paltry amount of interest. Since the federal government insures these deposits, as they do for savings accounts, there's no risk that you'll lose your money. It's also true that putting your short-term savings in a checking account will allow you to have the fastest access to your money, by withdrawing cash, writing a check, or using a debit card. However, the tiny amount of interest that's paid on these accounts makes them a poor choice for your savings.

• •

You may also want to consider an **online savings account** instead of a bank savings account. Online savings accounts offer the advantages of a bank savings account—convenience, quick access to your money, and federally insured deposits—but they pay significantly higher interest than bank savings accounts, and are sometimes even competitive with money market funds.

The sites that offer online savings accounts include ING Direct (www.ingdirect.com), Emigrant Direct (www.emigrantdirect.com), and GMAC bank (www.gmacbank.com). Some of these sites are actually full-service online banks; for example, ING Direct also offers online checking accounts, CDs, mortgages, and long-term investment accounts. Once you set up your account, you simply transfer money between your checking or savings account at your bank and your online account. (Although these sites are easy to use, you probably shouldn't keep your savings online unless you're comfortable using the Web.)

Before you choose an online savings account, do an Internet search to find all the options—you might search for "online savings account" or "high yield savings account." These search terms should also bring up online reviews of the various sites—be sure to read some recent reviews to find out what other savers think, since the accounts that offer the very highest interest rates may not have the happiest customers for other reasons. Also, as with any new account, check all the fine print before transferring your money.

Money Market Funds

A **money market fund** is a pool of conservative investments that are managed by a fund management company. The investments in the fund typically include certificates of deposit (CDs), US Treasury bills (bonds issued by the federal government), commercial paper (bonds issued by corporations), and other debt securities. Although money market funds aren't insured by the government, there's virtually no chance that you will lose your money in one of these funds.

You put your money into one of these funds by opening a **money market account**. These are like glorified checking accounts—you can write checks on your account, although you'll usually be required to withdraw at least $250 at a time. Usually there is a minimum balance that you need to keep in the account at all times. However, unlike CDs (see below), you can keep your account open indefinitely, and deposit or withdraw money from it as you go along.

For these reasons, a money market account is a good place to keep your emergency fund, as long as you can keep enough money in the account to avoid dipping below the required minimum balance (in which case you may be charged a fee). If you do need all your money for an emergency, you can withdraw it at any time—but once you do that, your account will be closed, and you'll need to wait to open a new one until you have saved enough for the minimum balance.

The interest that you'll earn on a money market account will fluctuate on a daily basis. In 2007 and 2008, the rates were running around 4% to 5%, but they were lower than that in the early 2000s, and much higher than that in the 1980s. Many companies offer money market funds; here are a few examples to get you started:

- Franklin Templeton Investments (www.franklintempleton.com; 800-632-2301)
- Fidelity (www.fidelity.com; 800-fidelity)
- AARP (www.aarpfinancial.com; 978-614-7600)
- TIAA-CREF (www.tiaa-cref.org; 800-842-2252)

Certificates of Deposit (CDs)

A **certificate of deposit (CD)** is a specific amount of money that you deposit for a certain time period in return for a fixed rate of interest. You can buy a CD for three months, six months, or one to five years from a wide range of lending institutions, including banks, savings and loans, and insurance companies. Here's an example of how a CD works: you buy a $1,000 one-year CD at 5% from your bank. At the end of one year, your bank pays you back $1,000 plus 5% ($50), for a total of $1,050. In general, the longer the period of the CD and the more money you invest, the higher the interest rate you can get.

Since CDs are insured by the government (up to $100,000, like savings accounts), they are risk-free—at least in theory. The only catch is that if you want to get your money back before the end of the term, you'll have to pay a penalty, and you may also lose some or all of the interest you've earned. As a result, CDs are much less flexible than money market funds, which allow you to withdraw your money at any time.

CDs can be a good option, as long as you use them for the right purposes. It doesn't make sense to buy a CD for your emergency fund, because you don't know when you'll need that money. However, you might consider using a CD to hold money that you want to reserve for an expense that you know will be due at a specific time, such as an insurance payment that is due six months or a year from now. (Just don't cut the timing too close, since it can take a few days to redeem your CD and process your payment.)

Before buying a CD, shop around for the best rate, and check the rates being paid by money market accounts. (If you find that money market rates are higher than CD rates, then a money market account is a better option.) You can call the banks and savings and loans in your area and ask about their current rates—or you can just check the financial section of your local newspaper, which may have already collected this information for you. (If you don't know where to find the information, ask for help at your local library.) You can also check the national rates posted at www.bankrate.com.

Short-Term Bond Funds

When a company or a government wants to raise money, it will issue **bonds**. A bond is basically an IOU—a promise to repay a certain amount to the owner of the bond on a certain date (the bond's maturation date). However, most small investors don't buy individual bonds; instead, they invest in a **bond fund**—a set of bonds that are chosen and managed by an investment company. (I'll explain bond funds more fully in chapter 14.) Funds that invest in short-term bonds are the final option we will consider for short-term savings.

Why Short-Term Bonds?

There are many kinds of bonds, as explained in chapter 14. However, for your short-term savings you should only invest in funds that focus on short-term bonds—those that are due to be paid back about one to four years from the issue date. You don't want to put any money you'll need soon in an intermediate or long-term bond fund, because the longer the time before the bond matures, the greater the risk that you could lose some money.

Although short-term bond funds are a fairly conservative investment, they are a bit riskier than either a money market fund or a CD. That's because the value of the bonds in the fund is likely to decline if the interest rate rises. However, over time, short-term bond funds should earn a bit more per year than money market funds or CDs. For this reason, short-term bond funds are only a good option for money that you won't need for a year or more.

Like a money market fund (but unlike a CD), many of these accounts allow you to write checks and take money out of your bond fund without paying a penalty.

In choosing a short-term bond fund, compare the fees charged, and be sure to pick a fund that has low fees, as described in chapter 14. Here are some short-term bond funds that are offered by large investment companies:

- Fidelity Short-Term Bond Fund (www.fidelity.com)
- Schwab Short-Term Bond Market Fund (www.schwab.com)
- T. Rowe Price Short-Term Bond Fund (www.troweprice.com)
- Vanguard Short-Term Bond Index Fund (www.vanguard.com)

To compare these funds, visit the Web site for each company. (You could also call these companies using the phone numbers listed under "Investment Information" at the bottom of table 12 in chapter 15.)

How to Get Started

As your short-term savings start to add up, you'll probably want to have a few of the savings options described above going at once, rather than relying on just one. For example, you might put your small savings deposits into an online savings account until they add up to enough to open a money market account. (Since bank savings accounts pay such low interest, don't leave your money in that kind of account for any length of time.)

Table 2 summarizes the major differences between the four short-term savings options. However, the information given in this table is just a rough guideline; the features described here may vary, and the relative rate of return among these options can change over time. For example, although this table indicates that CDs and short-term bond funds have a higher rate

Table 2. Short-term savings options

	Level of risk	Potential return	Early withdrawal penalty?	Deposits insured?	Check-writing privileges?
Savings accounts:					
Bank	None	Very low	No	Yes	No
Online	None	Low	No	Yes	Yes
Money market fund	Very low	Low	No	No	Yes
CD	None	Higher	Yes	Yes	No
Short-term bond fund	Low	Higher	No	No	Yes

of return than money market funds, this may not always be the case. Before you choose a savings option, be sure to research the current rates.

If you have never used any of these accounts before, I'd suggest that you start by putting some money into an online savings account or a money market fund, because these are the most flexible short-term savings options that offer a decent rate of return. If you have already established an emergency fund and are looking for the best return on some money that you know you won't need for at least a year, then consider buying a CD or investing in a short-term bond fund.

When you're ready to open a money market account or buy a CD, you could just visit your bank or credit union—they generally offer these options. However, I suggest that you shop around first. Banks typically offer lower interest rates than you can get elsewhere, and it may be well worth your time to find a financial institution that is offering higher rates.

I will explain how to open an account for a short-term bond fund in chapter 15. All the major mutual fund companies (including the four companies mentioned in table 12 in that chapter) offer both money market funds and short-term bond funds. In choosing a short-term bond fund, be sure to shop around and choose a fund that has low expenses.

Teach Your Children to Save

Most parents aren't doing a very good job of helping their children learn to manage their money. In a survey by FleetBoston of parents who had children age five or older, only 26% of the parents felt well-prepared to teach their kids about basic personal finances. Fewer than half of the parents felt they were a good role model for their children for saving and spending.[*]

As you know from working with children, whenever you teach a child something, you also learn a lot about the subject yourself. So one way to learn more yourself is to help your own children learn about money. The younger your children are, the easier it will be for

---

[*] FleetBoston, "Smarter Decisions with Fleet National Survey" (September 2003), www.cbanet.org/SURVEYS/literacy/Report.pdf.

them to accept what you're teaching them. You can start teaching your children about money as young as age 4, and you should definitely be teaching them by age 12. By age 13, many children have already developed their own (usually poor) money habits that will be difficult to change.

The typical approach to teaching children about money is to dole out a small sum each week. However, this practice actually just teaches children how to spend, not how to save or make responsible financial choices. Instead, consider giving your children more money less often, and let them make their own decisions about whether to spend this money or save it. The sooner your children learn how to handle money responsibly, the better prepared they will be when they are on their own.

There are some excellent online resources that can help you teach your children about money:

- Kids and Money: www.moneyinstructor.com/kids.asp

- Teaching Children Money Habits for Life: www.extension.umn.edu/distribution/ youthdevelopment/DA6116.html

- Money Savvy Generation: www.msgen.com

- Teach Your Children the Value of Money: www.finance.yahoo.com/how-to-guide/ family-home/12820

CHAPTER THREE

Get Out of Debt

Chapter Summary

This chapter explains how to reduce your debts. It describes the measures used to evaluate your creditworthiness. It explains why credit card debt is the worst kind of debt to carry and where to start in paying off your debts. It also discusses what to look for in a credit counseling service.

In our culture, too many people—including too many family child care providers—believe that it's perfectly acceptable to borrow money whenever they want something new, whether it be a car, a vacation, a computer, an appliance, or furniture. Many people also go further into debt by charging everyday items to their credit cards, such as food, gas, gifts, drinks, pet supplies, and clothing. The credit card habit has become so pervasive that it's easy to forget that whenever we charge something, we are actually borrowing money—and we may be charged a steep price for this service.

Most people today have never been taught the difference between acceptable debt and unacceptable debt. **Acceptable debt** is borrowing for something that will grow (appreciate) in value. **Unacceptable debt** is borrowing for something that will decrease in value.

Based on this guideline, the only things you should ever borrow money to purchase are a home, improvements to a home, and a college education. You should pay cash for everything else—and if you do decide to put some expenses on a credit card for the sake of convenience, you should pay off that debt in full at the end of each month to avoid having to pay any interest.

If this advice seems extreme or unrealistic to you, for now just think of it as a worthwhile goal to aim for. It's true that most people today don't think like this. I'm often asked, "Whoa! Are you saying that I should pay cash for my next car?" Yes, that's exactly what I'm saying. (And it can be done—I'll explain exactly how to set up a car replacement fund in chapter 6.)

Your Credit Rating

As we have seen, there *are* some legitimate reasons for taking out a loan. When those occasions arise, you will want to minimize the cost of your debt so that you will be able to pay it off as quickly as possible. Some people aren't aware that banks and other lenders don't charge everyone the same rate for the money they lend.

Whenever you try to borrow money—by applying for a loan or a credit card (or any other form of debt)—the lender will evaluate certain measures to assess how creditworthy you are—in other words, how likely you are to repay the loan on time. To do this, they will ask your permission to access your credit history and review your credit report and credit score. The more creditworthy they conclude that you are, the more money they will want to lend you, and the less they will charge you for that service.

Your **credit report** is a document that provides information about your credit history, including your credit card balances, loan balances, and any late payments. It also lists any inquiries that potential lenders have made into your credit history. These reports are compiled by the three major credit rating companies:

- Experian (www.experian.com)
- Equifax (www.equifax.com)
- TransUnion (www.transunion.com)

You're entitled to receive a free credit report from each of these companies during any twelve-month period. You can request all three of your credit reports at once, space them out throughout the year, or request them only when you need them. To order all three reports at once, you can visit www.annualcreditreport.com, or call 877-322-8228.

One thing your credit report *doesn't* include is your **credit score**, which is a number that creditors use to sum up your ability to repay your debt. Your credit score is based on the information in your credit report, distilled down to a single number that may determine whether your loan application will be approved, how much you can qualify for, and what annual percentage rate you will be charged. You can request your current credit score from the three credit rating companies for a fee.

There are various ways of calculating credit scores. For example, Equifax uses the FICO® credit score, which ranges between 300 and 850. However, since the three companies each use a slightly different system, a good score will vary slightly, depending on the system being used. Ask the credit rating company for more information.

A bad credit score may prevent you from obtaining the loan you need or raise the interest rate you must pay, making the loan less affordable and harder to pay off. A good credit score will allow you to get a loan when you need one, at a lower interest rate, so that the debt will have a smaller impact on your fixed expenses.

There are many ways to improve your credit score, but the most important one is to always pay your bills on time. If a lending officer sees any late payments in your credit report, she is likely to conclude that you're an unreliable borrower who may not be able to pay back the debt on time. To maintain a good credit score, only borrow money that you can easily repay, and make sure that you're living within your means.

Credit Card Debt

Credit cards are a convenience that makes it very easy to purchase items. However, if you are unable to pay off your credit card bill in full at the end of each month, this is a sign that you are overspending. Only 39% of the providers in our survey said that they were paying off their credit card bill at the end of every month—and their average monthly credit card balance was $5,084. Despite this, they clearly recognized the negative side of credit cards:

Pay off your credit card bills to avoid wasting money on interest payments. It makes everything you buy cost more.

Stay away from keeping up with your neighbors, and worry about yourself. Get out of credit card debt now!

Don't buy it unless you can pay cash for it. If your business can't support itself financially, taking on credit is not the answer.

I wish I had planned better and not gotten into using credit cards. Stay away from high-interest cards! I'm so relieved now that I'm finally seeing the daylight and am out from under my high-interest cards. I now have just one business credit card.

For most people, credit card debt is the biggest interest expense that they have to pay each month. Credit card interest is the worst kind of interest because the rates are so high—usually between 15% and 20%, but increasingly even higher than that. These very high rates make it difficult to pay off your debt, especially if you don't pay more than the minimum payment every month.

At an 18% interest rate, if you have a balance of $5,000 and make only the required minimum payment of $100 a month, it would take you over 30 years to pay off your balance—and your total payments would be $17,556! Yes, you read that right—you'd end up paying over three times the original amount that you charged.

Credit cards are tempting but deceitful—they offer a financial trap. In addition to the high interest rates, studies show that people tend to spend more if they use a credit card than if they pay by check or cash. Consider this typical scenario: you go to the store on Saturday morning to buy a toy that's on sale for 10% off, charging it on your credit card. When the credit card bill comes at the end of the month, you have other priorities, so you just pay the minimum balance. Depending on how soon you do pay your full balance, that toy is likely to end up costing you at least 5% to 10% more than the regular price (not the sale price) because of the interest on your credit card.

Another danger of credit cards is that it's very easy to get overextended, since you aren't paying the full price for your spending. If you start carrying high monthly balances or make any late payments, this will hurt your credit rating, which can lead to having to pay higher interest rates on your next mortgage, home equity loan, or car loan.

• •

Credit Won't Solve Your Financial Problems

As one of the providers quoted above said, if your business isn't making it financially, credit cards aren't the answer. Resist the temptation to use a credit card when you know you won't be able to pay off the bill that month.

If you're starting to have trouble paying your bills on time, take a serious look at reducing your spending, as described in chapter 1. Look for some ways to raise your income, as described in chapter 4. Make sure that you're collecting all your child care payments on time:

- Stop giving parents a grace period before they pay you.

- Require parents to pay you at least a week in advance.

- Make sure any parents in a government subsidy program are filing their paperwork on time to ensure you receive timely payments.

• •

How to Stop the Credit Card Habit

Carmen from California told me, "One day my husband and I realized that we weren't saving enough money for retirement, so we cut up all our credit cards except one that we use for major purchases." Sometimes the best way to control your credit card spending is to cut up all but one of your credit cards, and use that remaining credit card only for emergencies and major purchases.

I also suggest that you throw away any credit cards issued by individual retail stores or companies. You can also contact your credit card company and ask them to reduce your credit limit. However, *don't cancel any of your credit cards*, since this may have a negative effect on your credit score. Instead, just cut up the cards and stop using them.

Heidi from Wisconsin said, "I use cash to buy everything, because I spend less when I use cash than when I used a credit card." I suggest that you get into the habit of paying for things with good, old-fashioned *cash*—no checks, no credit cards. You may start thinking twice about spending your money as you peel off twenty-dollar bills for your next restaurant meal or new set of towels.

If you won't be able to pay off your credit card balance quickly, see if you can at least reduce the interest rate you're paying. Often you can negotiate a lower interest rate simply by calling your credit card company and asking for a lower rate! (That may be hard to believe, but it's true!) Tell the company that you'll switch your balance to another credit card unless they lower your rate—and often they will oblige. (Bear in mind that they are most likely to do this if you have made all your minimum payments on time.)

You may also be able to find another credit card company that's offering a lower rate by exploring some of the Web sites that compare the current credit card interest rates, such as www.creditcards.com, www.bankrate.com, or www.indexcreditcards.com. But even if you switch to another company, you'll still need to remain vigilant about the interest rate that you're being charged, since it may be raised at any time.

• •

Debit Cards

Debt cards aren't credit cards—when you use a debit card, the amount you charge is immediately deducted from the bank account that the card is linked to, so you aren't taking on any debt. Debit cards operate just like checks, except that there's no delay between using the card and the charge to your account (there's no "float").

Debit cards can be helpful in controlling your spending, since you can't run up debt from one month to the next. However, you do need to be careful with these cards, since even a small overdraft on your checking account can cause overdraft fees to start piling up on every check that is submitted to your account.

• •

How to Pay Down Your Debts

If you have a lot of debt, you may be wondering how you'll ever be able to pay it all off. For most people, paying off debt *is* possible, especially when you consider the alternatives (filing for bankruptcy or spiraling further and further into debt).

However, to succeed you'll need to stay very focused on reducing your spending, since the reason you got into debt in the first place is that you've been living beyond your means. Reforming your spending habits and paying off your debt aren't things that will happen overnight—they're long-term goals that will require patience and perseverance. However, many people have accomplished them, and you can too.

Preparing a business or personal budget is one step that you can take to help keep your spending down so you can pay off your debt; to learn how to create a budget for your business, see the *Family Child Care Business Planning Guide*. Here are some other resources that can help you further:

- *How to Get Out of Debt, Stay Out of Debt and Live Prosperously* by Jerrold Mundis

- *Credit Card Debt* by Alexander Daskaloff

- *Money Drunk, Money Sober: 90 Days to Financial Freedom* by Mark Bryan and Julia Cameron

- Debt Reduction Services Web site (www.debtreductionservices.org)

Prioritize Your Debts

To figure out where to start paying down your debts, make a list of all your debts according to the interest rate that you're paying, from the highest rate to the lowest. When you're done, your list might look something like table 3.

Table 3. List of debts by interest rate

Type of loan	Amount	Interest rate
Credit card	$5,300	18%
Home equity loan	$12,500	8%
Home mortgage loan	$174,000	7%
Car loan	$730	5%
Student loan	$3,600	4%

As a rule, it makes sense to pay off the loan with the highest interest rate first. However, if one of your other loans has a very small balance, you may want to consider paying that debt off first. This can give you a sense of progress and accomplishment—plus a few extra dollars to help pay down the next debt. (For example, in the above table, you might want to pay off the small balance on your car loan and then turn your focus to your credit card.)

Some people try to pay off their mortgage as fast as they can so that they won't have that burden every month. However, it actually makes more sense to pay off your credit card debt and any other high-rate loans first. Part of your mortgage debt is a tax-deductible business expense and the rest is a personal tax deduction (if you itemize on **Schedule A**). So it usually makes sense to pay off your mortgage and any home equity loans last.

So if you've been making an extra mortgage payment each month, congratulations—you've been trying to get out of debt! Just take that money each month and use it to pay down your credit cards instead.

Pay Off Debt or Increase Savings?

If your monthly fixed expenses include high debt payments, you may wonder whether you should try to save more money first or pay off your debts first. Although there's no "one size fits all" answer to this dilemma, as a rule you should try to address both of these major financial priorities at once, and not ignore either of them.

For example, don't put all your money into reducing your debt—if you do that, eventually you'll have an unexpected expense, such as a car repair, and you'll just have to increase your debt again to pay for it. To keep that from happening, you'll need to start building a short-term emergency fund while paying off your debts. Although this may slow your progress toward both goals, it is the more effective approach.

However, if you have high-interest loans, such as credit cards, it may be advisable to place a relatively higher priority on paying them off and a relatively lower priority on putting money toward your long-term savings—as long as you continue to put some money toward both of these goals every month.

Bear in mind that paying more toward your credit card debt will only make sense if you are able to stay out of debt. If you can do that, after you pay off your credit cards, you can use the money you were spending on credit card interest to make a larger contribution to your savings. However, if you tend to fall back into the habit of running up your credit card bill, it's better to follow a more balanced approach—keep making some contributions to your retirement and emergency savings each month, even if it takes you years to get your credit card debt under control. Don't postpone saving for your retirement!

• •

Filing for Bankruptcy

Filing for bankruptcy should be your very, very last resort for managing your debt. In 2005, changes to the bankruptcy laws went into effect that make filing for bankruptcy more difficult and expensive. If you file for bankruptcy, it may not wipe away all your debt, and the bankruptcy will remain on your credit report for many years, making it much more difficult to obtain any kind of loan—including a mortgage, home equity loan, car loan, or education loan (or to qualify for a credit card).

If you do think you need to consider filing for bankruptcy, consult an attorney to find out whether bankruptcy is an option for you under the new law. But working with a credit counseling service will usually be a better option than bankruptcy.

• •

Credit Counseling Services

If you're struggling to get out of debt, you may want to work with a nonprofit credit counseling service that helps people resolve their financial difficulties. A credit counseling service may be able to help you negotiate with your creditors and get lower interest rates, lower monthly payments, or reduced late charges. However, there is a wide range of quality in credit counseling services, so you'll need to choose a service very carefully. Some credit counseling services may not have your best interests as their primary goal.

Here are some guidelines for choosing a credit counseling service. This information is based on a booklet from the Enterprise Foundation called "Financing Family Child Care," which you can download as a free PDF file from www.enterprisecommunity.org/resources/publications_catalog/#child. (Also see the warning signs listed below.)

• Look for an agency that offers a range of counseling options, not just a debt management plan. The more options the agency offers, the more likely you are to get the kind of help you need. Ask the agencies you are considering if they offer budget counseling, savings and debt management classes, and other educational options.

• Find out all the costs involved. Although most agencies will offer similar deals from creditors to cut your debt, the fees involved may vary significantly. Find out what fees are charged when you open your account and what monthly fees, if any, you will have to pay after that. Get the full amount you will be charged in writing before you enroll.

- Bear in mind that just because an agency is nonprofit or affiliated with a familiar organization doesn't guarantee that it will offer high-quality services or have affordable fees.

- Demand high-quality, personalized service. The counselors in the agency should have taken full courses in credit, budgeting, and saving, not just a few weeks of training. The counselor should spend a good deal of time evaluating all your debts, not just your credit card bills. Find out how much training the counselors have received and how much personal service and one-on-one counseling you will receive.

- Ask about privacy and confidentiality. Make sure that the agency won't be selling or distributing any of your information to anyone else without your permission.

- Find out how the counselors are compensated. Ask a counselor directly if she will be paid more if she signs you up for a debt management plan. If she says yes, or if you feel as if you're being pressured to enroll with that agency, consider going elsewhere.

- Get the specifics on credit concessions. Find out exactly how much lower your monthly credit balance will be, and how long it will take to pay off your bills. Don't agree to a debt management plan until the agency has contacted each of your creditors and they have agreed to the plan you were offered.

Warning Signs

In choosing a credit counseling service, watch for these warning signs:

- If the setup fee for a debt management plan (also known as debt consolidation) is more than $50, and the monthly fees are more than $25, look for a better deal. If the agency is vague or reluctant to talk about the specific fees, go elsewhere.

- Some agencies claim that their fees are voluntary, but they will pressure you to pay their full fee, even if you can't afford it. Ask if the agency's fees are truly voluntary, and don't pay more than you can afford.

- Hang up on anyone who tries to give you a hard sell or seems to be "pushing" a particular debt savings plan.

- Any agency that offers you a debt management plan after spending less than 20 minutes looking at your finances hasn't taken enough time to understand your situation. The counselor should generally spend 30 to 90 minutes reviewing your finances, and then explain the options that would best meet your needs.

- The counselor should discuss with you whether a debt management plan would be appropriate for your situation, rather than just assuming that it is. If the agency doesn't offer any educational options, such as classes or budget counseling, consider another agency that does.

CHAPTER FOUR

Raise Your Income

Chapter Summary
This chapter describes ways to increase your income. It discusses in depth the options of caring for more children, raising your rates, and increasing your fees. It also explains a wide range of additional options that other providers have used successfully.

After learning how to reduce your spending, save more money, and get out of debt, the final step in getting a handle on your money is seeing if there are ways that you can increase your business profit. As one provider put it,

My first three years in business were the most difficult financially. I now consider my business successful because I'm able to pay all my bills on time, maintain a good budget, and keep up with improvements and repairs without using credit. I also have one full-time and one part-time employee. My program is at capacity three days a week, and I'm almost full the other two days. I also have a waiting list for infants. I've paid down my business loan by $26,000 in just under 23 months. I'm so proud of the high-quality care I provide—but I do wish I got paid more.

This provider is doing really well with the money management skills that we have discussed so far, but there is one more step that she can take. There are basically four approaches that you can take to increasing your income:

- care for more children
- raise your rates
- increase the fees you charge
- explore other ways to raise your income

What Should You Do with the Extra Money?
It's actually relatively easy to increase your income as described in this chapter. The trickier part is making sure you actually use that extra money to help achieve your financial goals.

I suggest that you resolve to dedicate a good part (or even all) of the additional income you raise to meeting your short- and long-term financial objectives. (The next chapter will explain how to set and prioritize your financial goals.)

Bear in mind that even a small amount can make a big difference. For example, if you earn $500 more this year from your annual rate increase, and you start putting that amount into a tax-deferred retirement plan every year, after 10 years you will have $7,243 in that account (assuming that your investment is earning 8% per year in a tax-deferred IRA).

Care for More Children

The single most important way to increase your income is to increase the number of paying children in your program. The family child care providers who earn the most money tend to care for the legal maximum number of children, or close to it. Most states will also allow you to care for more children if you hire an assistant. (For more information about the payback for hiring an employee, see chapter 8.)

Pat from Minnesota said that she tries to keep her enrollment at full capacity whenever possible. She reasons that if she's putting in 10 hours a day to care for 6 children, she might as well care for 8 children and contribute the extra money to her IRA. However, she also pays attention to the quality of the care she's offering, and she won't compromise her quality to expand her enrollment.

• •

Insurance Note
Before you increase the number of children in your program, talk to your homeowners and business liability insurance agents to make sure that you'll still be covered if you take on more children. Some policies limit the number of children you can care for, and others may raise your rates if you add more children.

• •

However, caring for more children may not be the best option for everyone. For one thing, you must follow your state licensing regulations—never take on more children than you're allowed to care for, or you will be operating illegally. Also, even if you *are* allowed to care for more children, it may not be the right decision for you:

• Make sure you don't lower the quality of your care by taking on more children. This could be an issue if you haven't planned carefully how to meet the needs of the new children you're adding.

• Hiring an employee to help you care for more children could be an option, but this isn't a simple decision. As we'll see in chapter 8, if you hire an employee, you may not make any more money unless you can care for at least three more children.

- Before caring for more children, consider whether this is something that you really want to do. The extra work may not be worth it to you.

Instead of taking on more full-time children, another strategy would be to care for more part-time children. If you set your rates properly, you should be able to earn more money caring for part-time children than full-time children. As a rule, the fewer number of hours a child is in care, the more you should charge per hour of care.

For example, if your regular weekly rate is $150 a week, then your daily rate for full-time children is $30 a day ($150 ÷ 5 days). If your program is open 10 hours a day, that means your hourly rate for full-time children is $3 an hour ($30 a day ÷ 10 hours). Your part-time rates should be higher than this. If you're asked to care for a child just 2 days a week, you should probably charge around $36 a day (20% more). If you're asked to care for a child for part of the day, your hourly rate should probably be around $5 an hour (67% more).

In this example, if you were able to fill one slot with two or more part-time children who were paying your daily rate, you would earn $30 more per week ($180 [$36 x 5] versus $150).

Of course, caring for part-time children has some disadvantages that may create more work for you and make it more difficult to manage your business. (That's why you should charge a premium for part-time care.) Although it is not impossible to manage part-time children—many providers do so successfully—you should be aware of some of the challenges involved:

- When you care for more part-time children, you have to keep track of scheduling everyone and make sure you don't exceed your licensing ratios.

- It may be very difficult to find part-time families who want to share one full-time slot in your schedule. For example, if you're caring for one part-time child from 8 AM to 1 PM, and another part-time child from 1 PM to 5 PM, you could easily become over-enrolled if the first child is picked up late or the second child is dropped off early.

- If you're able to find two part-time families to share one full-time slot and one of those families leaves, you may not be able to find another family that wants the same part-time schedule. If all your prospective new clients are looking for a full-time slot, you may have to let the remaining part-time family go. Not a fun choice.

Work Longer Hours

Working longer is another strategy for earning more money, perhaps by extending your program into evenings or weekends. Again, this is not for everyone. Most providers put in an eleven-hour day, and extending your hours further may seem like a terrible idea. However, there are some providers who work a second shift—and others who actually work 24 hours a day for at least some (or even all!) days of the week. (I'm always amazed to hear these stories; I don't know how these providers manage.)

If you do offer this option, your fees for evening and weekend care should be higher than your fees during the week, because this type of child care is hard to find. Check with your licensor to see if you are allowed to work longer hours, and talk to your business liability insurance agent and homeowners insurance agent to make sure you will still be covered. (If you work longer hours, some insurance policies won't cover you for the extra hours.)

• •

Work Less, Charge More?

Linda from California has five children of her own and a busy schedule. For years, she worked weekends to keep up with her business paperwork—preparing lesson plans, working on the children's portfolios, and refining her curriculum. In 2007, she decided that she wanted more time for herself, so she simultaneously raised her rates and cut her hours.

She raised her rates from $30 to $35 a day, and all the parents paid it. She also changed her closing time from 5:15 PM to 4:30 PM. Since she knew that some parents would have trouble adjusting to the new schedule, she allowed any client who asked for it to keep the later pickup time for one year. She used the 45 minutes she gained to complete the paperwork that she had previously been doing on weekends, giving herself more time with her family.

Linda says that she treats the children she cares for and their parents as part of her family, and she has a waiting list two years long.

• •

Raise Your Rates

Most family child care providers work very long hours and charge relatively little for it. (In fact, some providers charge only a token payment, or none at all, because they are helping relatives or other families who can't afford to pay more.) On an hourly basis, many providers make less than the minimum wage. (To learn how to calculate your hourly wage, see the *Business Planning Guide*.)

Most providers would probably say that they deserve to earn more than the hourly wage. However, the parents of the children in your care aren't going to voluntarily offer to pay you more (wouldn't that be nice!), so it's up to you to set your rates at a healthy level and keep raising them over time to keep up with inflation.

Many providers make the mistake of thinking that they have to keep their rates low to compete with other child care programs, but this isn't true. In general, day care centers charge more than family child care providers, yet every year more parents are choosing day care centers over family child care. The reason for this is that many parents *perceive* that these centers offer a higher level of care than a family child care provider. Therefore, it's essential that you continually let parents know how your program is offering high-quality care for their children.

If you are competing on the basis of quality, your rates should reflect this. The better the quality of your care, the higher your rates should be. As a general rule, if you're offering high-quality care, your rates should be in the top 20% of family child care programs in your area. (For detailed information about how to set your rates, see the *Family Child Care Marketing Guide*.)

- -

Will Raising Your Rates Increase Your Taxes?

I hear all kinds of reasons why providers don't want to raise their rates. One provider said to me, "I'm slow to raise my rates, because I don't want to pay more in taxes." Don't make this mistake! It's true that anytime you make more money, you'll pay more taxes. However, what's important is how much money you'll have after paying your taxes. When you increase your rates, you'll always end up with more money in your pocket *after* paying your taxes.

- -

Talking about Rates

Many providers feel uncomfortable discussing their rates with the parents of the children in their care. One provider expressed this fear well:

> *I would imagine that younger providers are earning the highest pay. Time and experience working with children should be a tremendous advantage, but I would bet that the older providers are actually paid the least. Not because we don't deserve it, but because we don't make the changes necessary to make sure we're paid according to our years of experience. It might be that we're thinking, "Will they still like me if I charge more?"*

Since you value your relationships with parents, you may feel reluctant to bring up the subject of money for fear of upsetting those relationships. The best way to discuss money is in the context of the quality of your care. You're providing a high-quality service, and if you're communicating this to parents by showing them how their children are growing and learning, it will be easier to talk about money.

Some providers are reluctant to charge more because they're afraid that the parents can't afford to pay more, so they will lose families. Of course, it's possible that you will lose a family when you raise your rates. This does happen. However, that won't be the end of the world. If you have set your rates at the maximum you can reasonably charge (as I suggest you do), then you can expect to occasionally lose a parent who doesn't want to pay that much for child care.

However, some of the providers who are afraid of losing a client have a long waiting list and haven't lost a dissatisfied family in years! In that case, how parents will respond just isn't an issue. If you have a long waiting list and no vacancies, you may be charging too little. Are you basing your rate on what you consider to be fair, or are you setting a competitive rate that reflects the demand for your program? If the first, then ask yourself, "What really *is* a fair rate?" I believe that it's fair for you to earn a reasonable standard of living by caring for other people's children—and other providers agree:

> *If you have a waiting list, raise your rates! You're in demand.*
>
> *Don't be afraid to charge the highest rate in your area.*
>
> *Charge an appropriate amount for child care; don't undersell your services.*
>
> *Don't be afraid to raise your rates, or to charge higher rates when you are just starting out.*
>
> *Be competitive with local day care centers. Call around and find out the rates they charge. Increase your rates yearly—it doesn't have to be by much.*

It's true that most parents won't be happy when you raise your rates, but in reality, the vast majority of parents won't leave just because you decide to raise your rates. (And if you view your job as solely making parents happy, then you should probably *lower* your rates!)

It may be easier to talk about rates if parents understand where their money is going. They may assume that you're making a lot of money—but the income you receive from them may be much higher than your actual business profit. To help them understand how much money it takes to run your business, you could share with them your hourly wage after expenses or show them a pie chart of your profit in relation to your expenses. For information about both of these options, see the *Business Planning Guide*.

Surprisingly enough, we find that the provider quoted at the start of this section is correct—new providers often do charge higher rates than more experienced providers. The reason for this is that new providers tend to be more aware of what the other local providers and day care centers are charging, and they tend to set their initial rates at the high end of the scale. But once their business is going, many providers are very reluctant to raise their rates, for all the reasons discussed above. If you're in that situation, the next question is, how can you start raising your rates?

• •

Your Money or Your Time?

Maybe you're getting by okay financially, and raising your income isn't your highest priority. In that case, instead of raising your rates you might consider getting more paid time off, by starting to charge for your vacations, for example. Although this wouldn't increase your income, it would give you more free time to spend with your family.

• •

How to Raise Your Rates

Some providers keep their rates unchanged so that they will never have to deal with the stress involved in talking about money with parents. Others intentionally charge less than the average rates in their area to help out low-income parents. However, as a rule your goal should be to set your rates so that they will reflect the quality of the care you offer and be competitive with the best programs in your community. To keep up as the local rates rise with inflation, this means that you will need to raise your rates on a regular basis.

It's true that many providers don't raise their rates for years—but that's exactly how more experienced providers end up earning less than someone who is just starting out. To make sure that you are being paid according to your years of experience, you should consider raising your rates annually. The easiest way to present this to parents is to add a new term to your contract:

Rates will be raised annually.

Rates will be raised annually in September.

Rates will be raised annually on September 1st by 2%.

Rates will be raised on the child's anniversary date each year, by no more than 3%.

Announcing this new term in your contract well in advance of your next rate increase will put the parents on notice and relieve much of the stress associated with raising your rates. When the time comes, if a parent objects to your rate increase, you can simply refer her to the contract that she signed. You don't have to give a reason for your annual increase, but if you think it would be helpful, you could explain:

My expenses (utilities, supplies, training, insurance, food) have gone up this year.

I have one more year of experience providing child care.

I have increased the quality of my program over the last year (bought new equipment, attended a training workshop, offered a new curriculum).

I have added more services (longer hours, more flexible pickup times, more field trips).

Adding an annual rate increase to your contract doesn't mean that you actually have to raise your rates every year. Let's say that one year you decide not to raise your rates for some reason. In that situation, don't let the date of your annual increase pass without explaining to the parents why you have chosen to skip it that year. You don't want them to think that you have dropped your annual rate increase policy. You might say, "This year I'm making an exception to my normal policy of raising my rates, since I had to close my program for several weeks due to an illness. However, next year I will follow my contract and raise my rates as usual."

Making it a practice to raise your rates annually will add up over the years and make a big difference in your income. If you're charging $140 a week and increase your rates by 3%, that will add up to $4.20 more per week per child. If you work 52 weeks a year, the difference that year will add up to $218.40 ($4.20 x 52) per child. If there are five children in your program, you will earn $1,092 more that year. If you raise your rates by another 3% the next year, you will earn an another $1,125. By raising your rates on an annual basis, you will have earned an additional $2,217 over two years.

And remember—if your spending and debt are under control, that additional $2,217 can go right into your retirement plan!

• •

You Don't *Have* to Raise Your Rates

In strongly recommending an annual rate increase, I don't mean to imply that every provider should raise her rates. If you're happy with your current payment arrangements, then I'm not suggesting that you make a change.

Many providers choose to keep their rates low because they want to serve low-income parents who can't afford to pay more. That is a commendable decision, and I salute your service to the community. You may not have the option of raising your rates. If you're receiving child care payments from a state subsidy program, you won't be able to set your own rates.

Since the government payments are usually lower than what you can charge private-pay parents, this creates a dilemma for providers who want to help low-income families but must make a financial sacrifice to do so. The solution to this dilemma is more public support for low-income families. You may want to work with your family child care association and other child care advocates to lobby for more federal and state support for low-income families.

• •

Collect Your Money on Time

It's not uncommon for a provider to fail to collect all the money that is owed her in a timely manner. This typically happens because the provider is reluctant to confront parents and enforce her contract. However, this practice can both hurt you financially and undermine your ability to enforce all your other rules. Don't allow parents to get behind in their payments. The best practice is to require parents to (a) pay for care at least one week in advance, and (b) pay for the last two weeks of care when they join your program. (For more information about these two rules, see *Family Child Care Contracts and Policies*.) Other providers agree:

> *Be firm with clients who try to cheat you out of your income—otherwise, this will keep putting you in the hole.*

All my child care is prepaid—that way I never have to be a bill collector, and I won't end up providing free care to deadbeats. No money = no child care. And all my clients are fine with this.

Educate Yourself; Offer High-Quality Care

As we have seen, the most important criterion for parents is the quality of the care their children receive, not its cost. Most parents are willing to pay more to get the peace of mind that they have found the best care provider for their children. For this reason, the most successful providers focus on improving their skills, the quality of their program, and the demand for their services. If you follow this strategy, at some point the rates that you charge will become a secondary issue. Here are some examples of different ways to make your program indispensable to parents:

- Bonna from Kentucky decided to approach raising her rates by raising the quality of her program. She became accredited by the National Association for Family Child Care, obtained the highest four-star rating of quality in her state, and was chosen as her state's family child care provider of the year in 2005. She is currently finishing work on her associate's degree. Bonna explains to parents what her program offers that they can't find anywhere else. She's also careful whom she accepts into her program, and the parents appreciate her efforts.

- Roxanne from North Dakota decided that she could earn more money and keep parents from leaving if she made her program more attractive. So she started a monthly newsletter for the parents, *Kids Care News*. Every month her newsletter contains thank-you notes, funny things the children say, notices for any days she will be closing early, program reminders (such as "bring warm clothing"), articles on parenting, and so on. Parents have told her that the newsletter has made the difference in deciding whether to stay with her program.

- Patty from Tennessee has been providing 24-hour care 7 days a week for over 20 years in a military community. She also earns extra money as a mentor for new providers, helping them plan their contracts and marketing strategies. After getting her associate's degree in early childhood development, she recently completed a bachelor's degree in business management. Next year she may start on a master's degree. "This is a career for me," she said, "it's not baby-sitting, and it's not a stopping-off point before I move on to something else. My husband spent 22 years in the Army—and my career is child care."

Increase Your Fees

In addition to raising your rates, you should also consider charging fees for as many of your services as possible. Since these fees aren't included in your rates, most parents won't take them into account when comparing the cost of your program with those of other programs. Also, it may be easier for you to add another fee or a paid vacation day than to raise your rates. On the other hand, you may think that some fees are just too petty to bother with, and not want the parents to feel as if they're being "nickel and dimed to death." So it's up to you to decide whether to raise your rates or increase your fees. (Whichever you choose, be sure to include a description of all your fees in your contract, and apply your fees consistently.)

The kinds of fees you charge are up to you—there's no right way or wrong way to set your fees. Nevertheless, I do recommend that you regularly review the fees that the other child care providers and centers in your area are charging and aim to remain competitive with them. (For an explanation of how to do that, see the *Business Planning Guide*.) In this section I'll discuss the most common child care fees. Although I'm not suggesting that every provider should charge every fee described below, I do believe that every provider should be charging at least *some* of these fees.

- **Late pickup fee**. Some providers give parents a grace period of five or ten minutes after the agreed-upon time to pick up their children. Others won't charge a late fee if the parent calls ahead to say she'll be late. However, if a parent picks up a child more than ten minutes late without calling ahead, I recommend that you charge her a late fee. Most providers do have a rule that they will charge a late fee, but some don't enforce it—and it doesn't make sense to have a rule if you don't enforce it! One way to make this rule easier to enforce is to prepare a bill for the late fee and just hand it to the parent when she shows up.

  Your late fees can also be a planned source of additional revenue. To illustrate this, let's look at two scenarios. Say that your pickup time is 5:30 PM, and you really don't want to work after that time. In that case you should set your late fee high enough to discourage parents from being late (you might perhaps charge $1 per minute). If one parent continues to be late, then you could raise your late fee just for that parent until it's high enough to change her behavior. (The highest late fee I've heard of—charged by a provider in North Carolina—is $10 a minute!)

  However, if you really would be willing to work after 5:30 PM for the right amount of money, then you'll need to set your late fee low enough that parents can still afford it and you can earn some extra cash. If you charged a late fee of a $1 a minute, you would earn $60 an hour, at least in theory—but few parents would be willing to pay that fee on a regular basis. If instead you lowered your late fee to, say $0.50 a minute, that would still be $30 an hour, but it would be much more affordable for parents. ("Parents—I'm having a sale on late fees, one-half off! See how much you can save!") If one parent is regularly 10 minutes late, twice a week, her late fees will add up to $10 a week, or $520 a year.

  If you prefer, instead of charging a late fee, you can just set a higher "evening rate" after 5:30 PM. That approach eliminates the sense of penalty and guilt that is associated with paying a late fee, making it even more likely that parents will take advantage of it—and that you will earn a bit more money.

- **Registration fee.** Before a child is enrolled in your program, you're likely to spend a lot of time with the family and doing paperwork—and most providers don't charge for this time. This includes the time you spend on initial phone calls with the parents, your interview with them, and the paperwork needed to update your licensing records, your own records, and the contract for the new family. Many day care centers do charge a registration fee to offset the time required for these tasks, and it may make sense for you to do so, as well. As of 2008, registration fees are usually about $25 to $50.

- **Re-registration fee**. If you do charge a registration fee, a re-registration fee is also appropriate each year to cover the time you will need to spend updating your records, licensing forms, and client contract. You could also tell parents that this fee helps to offset the cost of the annual license or inspection fees that you must pay to maintain your child care license. Some states, including California and Minnesota, will pay you an annual re-registration fee for children whose parents are eligible for the state subsidy program. (In some states, these fees aren't in addition to the regular subsidy payment.)

- **Returned check fee**. If your bank returns a parent's check due to insufficient funds, you'll have to pay your bank a fee. It's reasonable to pass this fee on to the parent and also add to it your own returned check fee ($25 is common) to cover the inconvenience to you and the time you have lost dealing with the matter.

  If you normally keep a relatively low balance in your checking account, you run a risk that one bounced check from a parent may cause many of your own checks to be returned. In this situation, the bank's fees on your account can spiral upward alarmingly fast, especially since it may be a few days before you even find out that the parent's check was returned. To cover this, I suggest that you include a term in your contract stating that if a parent writes you a bad check, the parent will be responsible for all the resulting bank fees, including all fees for any checks returned to your account.

- **Holding fee**. Sometimes a parent will want to start his child in your program at a certain point in the future—for a newborn or a child returning from summer break. In this case, you shouldn't guarantee that you will hold a space for the child unless the parent pays you to hold that space. You should charge a holding fee in exchange for your promise not to fill the space before the desired starting date. The fee you charge for this service can be a flat amount, half your regular rate, or your full rate. In fact, you can charge whatever you wish. However, if the parent doesn't want to pay your holding fee, then don't promise to hold the space. Tell the parent that you will be happy to enroll the child if you still have an opening when the child is ready.

  I also don't recommend that you apply the holding fee toward child care once the child is in your program. This fee is intended to reimburse you for the loss of income that you incurred by holding the space open. Therefore, state in your contract that this fee is nonrefundable. Also, don't make the mistake of holding a spot for a "deposit" that will be applied to the last week of care. The parent may decide not to join your program and then demand that you return her "deposit." This would create an unnecessary dispute.

- **Field trip fee**. Field trips are a great way to expose the children in your care to new learning opportunities. These trips can be as simple as a walk around the block or as exciting as a trip to the zoo, a museum, or an amusement park. If you incur expenses on a field trip—gas, entrance fees, food or treats, an extra helper—you might consider passing these costs on to the parents.

    Tiffany from Illinois told me that she realized she had been spending a lot of money (for lunch, entrance fees, gas, and so on) when she took the eight children in her care on field trips—so she changed her practice. Now she estimates the cost of each field trip in advance and then charges the parents a fee to cover it. For a recent trip to the Children's Museum, she calculated in advance that the cost per child would be $12.50, including lunch, one souvenir per child, the entrance fee, and the gas for her car.

- **Damage fee**. Although it's normal for children to break toys and perhaps small items around your home, you can set a limit on what you are willing to pay for repairs. Certainly you shouldn't pay for any damage to toys or other items that a child brings to your program from home. If a child causes damage that's beyond what you think is reasonable, then you should ask the child's parents to pay for it. For example, if a child breaks your television or recklessly breaks a window, you should consider asking the parents to repair the damage. (Never punish a child for any damage she has caused by accident.)

    Bear in mind that you want to avoid making small claims for these kinds of repairs on your homeowners policy, since this can cause the insurance company to raise your rates. However, it's possible that the parent's homeowners insurance may cover the damage, if the parent chooses to file a claim on his insurance policy.

- **Liability insurance fee**. You will need to carry a business liability insurance policy to protect yourself against the risks involved in running a family child care business. The amount of insurance you buy should be based on what you can afford—but the more coverage you can get, the better. (For a list of the insurance policies that all providers should carry, see the *Business Planning Guide*.)

    Since your business liability insurance also covers any injuries to the children in your care, it isn't unreasonable to ask parents to share the cost of this insurance with you. If your premium on this insurance is due twice a year, then you might pass on some of this cost to the parents every six months when your premiums are due.

- **Curriculum fee**. Many providers use a commercial child development curriculum to help them plan the learning activities for the children in their care. You could charge parents a fee to cover the cost of this curriculum.

- **Charge for absences**. Twenty years ago it was more common for providers to charge parents by the hour than by the week. But times have changed—now the ratio has reversed, since more providers are relying on their income to support their family. Except for some rural areas, most providers now charge by the week or the month, not by the hour. This means that you're providing a guaranteed service and reserving a set amount of time each week for a specific child.

If a child doesn't show up one day, you have still set aside the time to care for that child, and you should be paid for it. (There are many services that we pay for whether we use them or not—rent, newspaper and magazine subscriptions, cable television service, and so on. College students still have to pay tuition even if they skip all their classes.) For all these reasons, it's reasonable to require parents to pay for your services, whether the child comes to your program or not. Some providers do allow parents to take a few unpaid "sick days" each year. Although this is common, you don't have to do it.

Charging for your own "absences" is a different matter. If you aren't able to provide care because you're sick, then you may not want to charge parents for those days.

- **Charge for vacations and holidays**. The vast majority of working parents get paid for their vacations and holidays, but most family child care providers do not. This shouldn't be—and fortunately, providers are increasingly charging for at least some of their vacation and holiday time. (You can charge for the vacation time that your clients take as well as the vacations that you take yourself.) I believe that all providers should set a goal of being paid for two weeks vacation and all eight major federal holidays.

  As Kalissa from Iowa told me, "I had only been in business a year when I attended a family child care association meeting where they told us that to be a professional we needed to charge for vacations and holidays. I went home and revised my contract to add seven paid vacation days and nine paid holidays. None of the parents objected to paying for those additional days."

  If you don't yet charge for vacations or holidays, you may want to introduce them slowly, a few extra paid days each year. If you care for four children and your weekly rate is $130, a week of paid vacation will add $520 to your income each year. If you also take four paid holidays (Christmas Day, New Year's Day, Thanksgiving, and the Fourth of July) this will add up to another $416 each year ($26/day x 4 children x 4 holidays = $416).

  If you prefer not to charge directly for your vacations and holidays, you might consider doing so indirectly, as this provider did:

  I took three weeks of unpaid vacation last year, but I adjusted my weekly fee for the other 49 weeks to make up for the lost revenue during those three weeks. That approach felt better to me, and the families felt okay if they had to hire another provider when I was off. No one said, "Hey, I don't get three weeks off."

- **Charge for your professional days**. Most states require providers to take training workshops to maintain their license. Some providers also attend classes to obtain a professional credential, such as National Association for Family Child Care accreditation, a Child Development Associate (CDA), or a postsecondary degree in early childhood development. It's a growing trend to charge parents for at least some of the days that you take off to further your education.

More Strategies for Increasing Your Income

Let's say you have expanded your program to its optimal size, added a contract term that you will raise your rates annually, and implemented all the fees that you're comfortable charging—and you'd still like to earn more. Don't worry—there are many, many more ways to increase your income. This fourth section is a grab bag of a wide range of ideas that either I would recommend or other providers have told me about.

- **Charge higher rates for infants**. Infant care is typically the most difficult kind of care for parents to find because of the high demand and the limited number of infants a provider is allowed to care for. For this reason, your fees for infants should be much higher than your fees for toddlers and preschoolers. However, many providers don't take advantage of this reality; they charge only slightly more for infants than for older children. Use the infant rates charged by the day care centers in your area as a model for what you could be charging. Many providers offer high-quality infant care in a setting that is highly desirable to parents. If you're reluctant to raise your overall rates, consider just raising your rates for infants.

- **Don't offer multiple-child discounts**. Some parents may ask you for a discount on your rates for a second child from the same family. However, I don't recommend that you agree to this, since it won't cost you any less to care for the second child. Also, the cost of a permanent discount will add up and significantly reduce your income over time. Instead, consider offering the parents a short-term discount for six months or so.

- **Collect copayments from subsidized families**. If you charge your private-pay parents more than the amount the state pays you for subsidized child care, in many states you are allowed to ask the parents for a copayment to make up the difference. (Check with your subsidy program case worker to find out if your state allows you to ask for a copayment.)

    Some providers don't try to collect these copayments because the parents are struggling financially. However, you shouldn't feel ashamed to ask for a copayment. Low-income parents must meet their other obligations to pay for food, rent, and clothing—and child care expenses are no less important. If your state allows it, ask the parents to make their copayments in advance so that you will be assured of getting all the money that is owed you.

    Also, educate yourself about the rules for your state's subsidy program, and make sure that low-income parents are submitting their paperwork on time.

- **Claim higher subsidy payments**. Some state subsidy programs will pay you a higher rate for child care if you have achieved a professional or educational credential, such as a CDA, NAFCC accreditation, or a postsecondary degree in early childhood development. For example, in Minnesota a provider is paid 15% more if she has one of these credentials. This extra payment can be a financial boon—if you normally receive $130 per week per child from the state subsidy program, an extra 15% would mean $19.50 more per week, or $1,014 more per year, per child. If you care for five children in the subsidy program, this would add up to an extra $5,070 per year.

• •

Bartering for Child Care

Some providers exchange child care for services from a parent, such as car repair, chiropractic care, or home improvements. Bear in mind that there is no financial benefit for bartering, since for tax purposes both parties must treat the transaction as if money had changed hands. In other words, you have to report the value of the services you received in exchange for child care as if it were cash income. For this reason, bartering won't save you any money. However, it can help you get the services you need in a convenient way as well as strengthen your relationship with the families in your program.

• •

- **Get a second job**. More than one provider in our survey said that she had another job to help make ends meet. As one put it, "Don't depend on family child care alone! Even as a long-term, accredited provider, I can't make enough money to run a quality program and meet my financial needs." However, this doesn't mean that you need to serve hamburgers; here are some examples of the jobs that other providers have:

  - Bonna from Kentucky works as a trainer for her state, teaching other providers how to improve their environments, policies, and procedures.

  - Olga from California works as a teacher for early childhood mentors. She works in a program that trains local college students who are studying early childhood education and receives a stipend each semester. She has the students come to her home, where she evaluates their art activities, circle time activities, and other projects.

  - Loretta from Indiana works a second job at an auction service, working 8 to 12 hours every Sunday and from 6 PM to midnight, 2 nights a week. She originally took this second job to pay for the college education of her two children, but she has kept at it to fund her retirement. She also holds a fund-raiser twice a year for her program. She and the parents sell candles, and she earns about $1,000 each time. She uses this money to buy playground equipment for her program.

- **Participate in the Food Program**. Every provider should join and participate in the Food Program. This is both a significant source of income and a resource that will help you serve nutritious food to the children. Some providers mistakenly believe that they will be better off financially if they don't join the Food Program, but this is just wrong. Your deduction for food expenses will be the same regardless of whether you participate in this program or not. But you will be better off if you are participating, since the reimbursements from the program will increase your income. For more information, see the *Family Child Care Record-Keeping Guide*, 7th Edition.

- **Claim all your tax deductions**. To increase your income, be sure to claim all the allowable deductions on your federal tax return. For every $100 of business deductions that you claim, your taxes will go down by $30 to $45, depending on your tax bracket. Check your return before you file—Have you deducted all the meals and snacks you served to the children? Did you record all the miles you drove your car for business purposes, including trips to the bank, library, grocery store, garage sales, and so on? Have you saved your receipts for household expenses, such as light bulbs, laundry detergent, and paper towels? Every deduction counts. For a list of more than 1,000 allowable deductions, see the *Record-Keeping Guide*.

- **Charge for photographs of the children**. Some other money-making ideas begin with taking digital photos of the children during the day. You can e-mail the photos to the parents and charge them a fee if they want a printed copy of any of the photos. (The fee should cover your time, as well as your printer supplies.) Another idea is to prepare a photo album for a child's birthday (or when the family leaves your program), and charge a fee for this service.

- **Hold a fund-raiser**. There are a number of companies that offer you the opportunity to sell products to earn money. In addition to the familiar Tupperware parties, these products include candy, frozen pizza, and other frozen food. You can explain to the parents that you're raising money for a special purpose, such as a field trip, a training workshop, or new playground equipment, and encourage them to sell these products to their friends and family. For example, Sue from Indiana has held several Tupperware parties with the help of the parents in her program, and each time she has made $100 to $200. She also sells Discovery Toys to get free toys for her program.

- **Hold a garage sale**. Schedule a garage sale to raise funds for your program, and ask parents to contribute items for you to sell. Explain to them that you're trying to earn enough to buy a specific item needed in your business, such as a computer or toys.

- **Offer lessons to the children**. Add the option of swimming lessons, ballet lessons, piano lessons, gymnastics, or other classes to your program, and charge parents for these lessons. If you don't have the qualifications to teach the class, bring in an outside teacher. When setting your fees for the lessons, add a markup in addition to what the teacher is charging you. To justify this, remember that you are providing a big benefit for the parents, since they won't have to arrange the lessons with the teacher or drive the child to and from each lesson themselves.

- **Provide extra services to parents**. Poll the parents to see if they are interested in paying for any additional services that you might be able to offer. This might include providing a diaper service, cutting the children's hair, making a homemade family dinner for parents to take home when they pick up their child, photographs of the children, or various kinds of lessons (as described above).

- **Stay happily married**. Most of the family child care providers in this country are married. In our survey, 82% of the providers were married, 14% were single without a partner, and 4% were single with a partner. If you're married, your spouse's income may be what is making it possible for you to stay in business. "I wouldn't have continued in day care if my husband didn't have a good job," said one provider. Another commented, "Unmarried providers have the biggest financial difficulties. Unfortunately, a child care business really cannot support a family."

  Although a family with only one income may be at a disadvantage, some family child care providers wouldn't agree with that last statement. There are many providers who do support a family on their income. And it actually is possible to make good money as a child care provider—say, $90,000?

• •

It *Is* Possible: The Provider Who Earned $90,000 in Her First Year

Although most providers earn a modest income, one provider in Florida earned over $90,000 (before expenses) in her first full year in business. How did she do it?

- She cared for the maximum number of children allowed under state law (10).

- She specialized in part-time children (so she actually cared for 70 children).

- She hired an assistant to help her.

- She joined the Food Program.

- She charged her private-pay parents about double the county subsidy payment, and required the subsidized parents to pay the difference.

- She didn't give any discounts to multiple children from the same family.

- She offered care for shift workers, and her program was open for 24 hours, Monday through Friday.

- She offered drop-in care at $10 an hour.

- She raised her rates twice in her first year so that they ended up matching the most expensive day care center in her area by the end of the year.

At the end of the first year, she had a waiting list and was receiving multiple inquiries every day for her services. Her goal for the next year? $100,000!

• •

CHAPTER FIVE

Set Your Financial Goals

Chapter Summary
This chapter describes how to prioritize your short-term and long-term financial goals. It lists the seven financial goals that all providers should consider, in order of importance. It explains how to develop a plan for meeting your financial goals to help you stay focused on the long term.

While flying over the ocean, you suddenly hear the pilot's voice over the intercom—"Hi, folks! I've got some good news and some bad news. The good news is that we're making great time. The bad news is that we're lost." Meeting your financial goals can be like taking a long plane trip—to reach your destination, you need to know where you are headed and stay on course. This means that you'll have to identify your goals and your time frame for meeting them so that you can make the choices needed to reach each goal on time.

Your financial goals will include both your short-term goals for the next one to five years and your longer-term goals, such as saving for retirement or college. Your short-term goals might include paying off your credit cards, saving for a down payment on your first home, or buying a car with cash. (Chapter 2 explained the options for saving money toward your short-term goals. Part III will discuss in detail how to invest your savings to meet your long-term goals.)

Prioritize Your Goals

To achieve your financial goals, you'll also need to prioritize them—just as a pilot needs a flight plan that tells her which cities to fly to, in what order. Meeting your financial goals will require patience and perseverance, since doing so may take longer than you'd like—especially to reach your long-term goals. It can be very difficult to stay focused on your long-term goals when other short-term needs keep popping up. The way to stay focused on what you need to be doing at any given time is to **prioritize** your goals. This simply means making a list of your financial goals in their order of importance to you.

Although you'll need to decide the level of importance for each of your own goals yourself, there are some guidelines that I think you should consider. To explain them, in this chapter I'll discuss the seven financial goals that are essential for most people, in the order that I recommend you work on them. This list may not include all the goals on your own list, but you should make sure that your list does include each of these goals that applies to you. In order of importance, here's my list:

1. Contribute enough to a 401(k) or 403(b) retirement plan to get the full employer match.
2. Buy adequate insurance.
3. Pay off your credit card debt.
4. Establish a three-month emergency fund.
5. Establish a car replacement fund.
6. Save at least 10% of your profit for retirement.
7. Save for your children's college education.

1. Get the Employer Retirement Match

If you or your spouse works for a company that offers a 401(k) or 403(b) retirement plan and matches some of the employee contributions to that plan, it's vital that you contribute enough to the plan to receive the full employer match. Typically, the maximum match will be 1% to 3% of the employee's salary. For example, let's say your spouse earns $40,000 a year and his employer offers a 2% match. This means that if your spouse contributes 2% of his salary ($40,000 x 2% = $800) that year, his employer will match it by contributing another $800. Therefore, at the end of the year the balance in the plan will be twice as much as your spouse contributed ($1,600).

Meeting any employer match that is available to your family should be your number one financial priority, since there is no other investment you can make that will immediately double your money like this.

2. Buy Adequate Insurance

Even if you take all the commonsense steps you can to run a safe program, providing child care in your home will expose you to an increased risk of lawsuits, property damage, and accidents. After taking steps to keep yourself and the children safe, the next thing you can do to reduce your risks is to purchase adequate insurance. You will also want to make sure you have health insurance, life insurance, and long-term care insurance for yourself and your family.

For more information about buying insurance, including the kinds of insurance that you should carry to cover your business risks and the amount of coverage you should carry, see the *Family Child Care Legal and Insurance Guide*.

3. Pay off Your Credit Card Debt

If you are carrying a high burden of credit card interest, this can make it very difficult to reach any of your other financial goals. For a full discussion of credit card debt and how to pay it off, see chapter 3.

4. Establish an Emergency Fund

Are you prepared to deal with an unexpected $1,000 expense? Life is full of unexpected events; for example,

- Your car breaks down and requires a major repair.
- You fall and break your arm, and are unable to provide child care for four to six weeks.
- A flood damages your home, forcing you to shut down your business for two months.
- Your mother becomes ill, and you leave town to stay with her until she recovers.
- The largest employer in town shuts down, and three families tell you they are leaving.

If you think about it, unexpected events are such a fact of life that we really should call them *expected* events. Since you're almost guaranteed to encounter a major financial disruption at some time in the next few years, you should plan ahead by setting aside at least three months of living expenses in an emergency fund. Deposit this money in a money market fund or another short-term option where it can be easily accessed (as explained in chapter 2). Here's what other providers say about their emergency funds:

> *After five years of struggling, the best thing I did was to put six months' worth of living expenses into a savings account. This completely changed the way I did business, because I didn't have to worry about the money factor when making business decisions about terminating or enrolling new children.*

> *Make sure you have a three-month emergency fund before you spend any money on more supplies—and I actually feel you need more than three months. My goal is to have a six- to eight-month backup fund. Because we have those reserves, if a family doesn't work out, I can feel okay letting them go.*

> *I think it's important for child care providers to have a plan B—a backup plan. Plan for bad weather, power outages, becoming ill and not being able to work, and car breakdowns and repairs. Think of everything you can that could affect your income, and develop a backup plan that will help offset the loss of income in those situations.*

5. Establish a Car Replacement Fund

Ideally, you should aim to pay cash the next time you buy a car or van. Otherwise, the interest you'll have to pay on the car loan will significantly reduce your ability to save more money. You can prepare to pay cash for your next car by putting aside some money each month. To find out how to establish a car replacement fund, see chapter 6.

6. Save at Least 10% of Your Profit for Your Retirement

In chapters 11 and 12 I'll explain how to estimate how much you should be saving for your retirement now. The most important thing to understand about saving for retirement is that the sooner you start, the easier it will be to build a comfortable retirement fund. Next year isn't soon enough—every year counts! If you start saving while you're in your twenties or thirties, saving 10% of yearly profit may be enough. However, if you wait until you're in your forties or fifties, you'll need to save much more of your profit each year to provide yourself with enough income to retire without financial stress.

7. Save for Your Children's College Education

You may be surprised that saving for your children's college education is so low on this list of financial priorities. The reason for this is that there are many ways to pay for college, including scholarships, work-study programs, grants, and loans. (In comparison, you can't borrow the money you need to pay for your insurance or retirement savings.) In addition, your children will be able to share the responsibility for their college expenses with you.

Note: If you're saving money for your own college education, then I'd suggest that you place this financial goal much higher on your list—perhaps in third or fourth position. A college education is an important investment that will have a significant financial payback over the course of your life.

• •

Don't Forget to Invest in Yourself

Your greatest financial asset is your own earning power. One way to improve that power is to set up a professional development plan and take time each year to improve the skills needed to run your business. This might include getting more training in child development, business finances, record-keeping, or communicating with parents. For more information, see the *Business Planning Guide*.

To preserve your earning power, you also need to take care of your physical health and emotional well-being. Some providers take one or more personal days each year to relax and reduce their stress level. Bear in mind that you should be enjoying your work! If you aren't, then you may want to reconsider your options and see if you can find another career that will make you happier.

• •

Develop a Financial Plan

Don't worry if you haven't yet met all the goals outlined above—very few people have (which is why I'm listing them as goals). What's important is that you set your own financial goals and develop a plan for how you will meet them over time.

Here's an example of how you might plan and balance your priorities: you decide to start contributing to your spouse's 401(k) plan right away, while also focusing on paying off your credit card debt within the next two or three years. Since you can't afford to set aside a full three months of living expenses right now, you set a goal that you will start to contribute $100 a month to an emergency fund at the end of the year, when you expect to pay off your first credit card.

You'll reach your goals more quickly if you establish the habit of making some progress toward them each year. Any progress—even if it's slow—is better than no action at all. Once you prioritize your goals and set a target date for each one, you'll be able to incorporate these financial objectives into your annual budget. (To learn how to prepare a budget for your business, see the *Business Planning Guide*.)

Plan for the Long Term
Don't let yourself feel overwhelmed by this list of financial priorities. I'm not suggesting that you should save every last penny you have for the future and not be able to enjoy your life today. However, I am encouraging you to take your long-term financial goals seriously, and to make them a higher priority than some of your current discretionary spending. Each time you're thinking of buying something, stop and ask yourself whether this purchase really is all that important in light of your other financial priorities.

At the end of each year, review the progress you have made toward your goals that year. Don't be discouraged if your progress has been slow—just keep at it. As you become more comfortable addressing your financial goals, you'll gain more control over your spending and reduce the stress you feel about money. As you make progress toward these goals, you'll start to feel a sense of freedom and relief that will make all your hard work worthwhile!

Carmen from California knows that she isn't saving enough for retirement. But she told me that her family's financial health will improve in the next year because "we're determined to make it better." Regardless of your current income, if you're focused on improving your finances and planning for the long term, you'll be more likely to find ways to save money and improve your situation. So don't dwell on how little you have saved in the past; instead, focus on the future. Remember, it's *never* too late to start saving.

PART II

Understand Your Options

CHAPTER SIX

Buying a Car or Van

Chapter Summary
This chapter examines six key financial issues involved in buying a car or van.
It will help you decide how to choose your next vehicle and how much to spend
on it. This chapter also explains how to set up a vehicle replacement fund so
that you will be able to pay cash or borrow less for your next vehicle.

Most family child care providers use a vehicle in operating their business. You might
use your car or van to transport the children on a regular or occasional basis, taking them to
school or transporting them on field trips. You probably also use it for business errands, such
as driving to the bank to deposit your business income, going to garage sales to find toys
and play equipment, and driving to the store to buy food and business supplies.

When it comes time to start thinking about replacing your vehicle, don't proceed until
you have thought through the financial implications of the following questions:

- How much money should I spend?
- Should I buy a new or used vehicle?
- Should I buy or lease my new vehicle?
- Should I spend more to get a bigger tax deduction?
- How will I pay for the new vehicle?
- How will my decision affect my vehicle insurance?

The rest of this chapter will discuss these questions in depth to guide you in both buying a
new car or van and preparing for that purchase by setting up a vehicle replacement fund.

How Much Should You Spend?

Our culture glorifies the car. We're regularly subjected to million-dollar advertising cam-
paigns designed to convince us that we need to own a fancy, expensive vehicle to meet our
emotional needs—"freedom," "fun," "power," "comfort," "sex," and so on. We have lost
sight of the real reason for buying a car—the functional need to get from one place to the
next. As a result, many people buy vehicles that are too large and expensive for their needs.

It's true that providers who regularly use their vehicle to transport a lot of children may need an SUV or van. It's also reasonable to buy a more expensive vehicle on the basis of higher ratings for safety and reliability. Nevertheless, many providers still spend more than they need to.

To get the most economical vehicle, you should buy a high-mileage, reliable car, and hold onto it for as long as possible. Resist the urge to trade it in after just three to five years. Have the car regularly serviced, and keep it clean to reduce your maintenance costs. To find the best car for your needs, check the buying guide and reliability ratings listed in *Consumer Reports*—look through past issues of the printed magazine at your local library, or check the information posted on the Web site www.ConsumerReports.org.

Should You Buy New or Used?

As a rule, you'll spend less on transportation over time if you buy a used vehicle instead of a new one. As described above, the temptation to buy a new vehicle is very strong in our society. Many people see a new car as a status symbol and an expression of their self-esteem. However, buying a new car can also be a waste of money.

A new vehicle does offer the advantage of a warranty that will cover you if the vehicle's parts fail. However, your brand-new vehicle will lose a great deal of its value as soon as you drive it off the dealer's lot. Also, the cost of insurance will be higher for a new vehicle than for a used one. It's true that the interest rates for new cars are usually a little lower than they are for used cars—but if you follow my advice (see below), you'll be able to minimize the amount you'll need to borrow.

If you use your vehicle to transport children, then you won't want to buy a car that isn't reliable and might break down. You also won't want to have to spend a lot of time and money maintaining the vehicle. However, you can get a used vehicle that's just a few years old and in good condition.

Before you buy a used vehicle, ask to bring the car or van to your own mechanic for inspection to ensure that it's safe to drive, especially for carrying children. This step can save you a lot of money on repairs and maintenance, since it can greatly reduce your chances of buying a lemon.

• •

Check the Car's History
You can find out the history of any used vehicle you are considering at www.carfax.com. This Web site will research the car's vehicle identification number (VIN) and check if its history has any red flags that should give you pause. For example, carfax will tell you how many owners the vehicle has had, whether it has ever been a fleet car, whether it has ever been in an accident or a flood, or whether it has ever been rebuilt or stolen.

• •

Should You Buy or Lease?

When you buy a car, it's yours—you own it (along with the bank, if you took out a loan to buy it). When you lease a car, you must return it at the end of the lease. Leasing is attractive to some people because it allows them to get a more expensive car for the same monthly payment. The reason the monthly payments are lower is that when you lease, you only have to pay for the vehicle's depreciation, not its full purchase price. However, if you are in an accident and damage a leased car, you could be socked with extra charges (since it's not your property).

Leasing can also be attractive because the up-front costs are lower. However, the long-term costs of leasing are usually higher than the costs involved in buying a car. So the shorter the period of time you plan to use the car, the more sense it might make to lease. Having said that, I will add that leasing is primarily for people who want to drive a more expensive car than they can afford to buy. For this reason, I don't recommend that you lease your vehicle. (Also, if you have bad credit, it will be easier for you to get a loan for a new car than to be approved for a lease.)

If you do decide to lease, closely examine all the actual costs over the term of the lease that are outlined in the contract. Bear in mind that paying cash to buy a vehicle will always save you the most money because you won't be paying extra for loan interest or leasing costs.

Should You Spend More for the Tax Deduction?

When you use a vehicle in your business, you're entitled to claim some of the cost of operating the vehicle as a business expense. Knowing this, some providers believe that they'll get a bigger tax deduction if they spend more when they lease or buy their next vehicle. Does it make sense to spend more money to get a bigger tax deduction? The answer is no!

When managing your money, reducing your taxes as much as possible is not the ultimate goal. The ultimate goal is having more money *after* you pay your taxes. There's a big difference! Here's an example to show you what I mean:

Let's say you have narrowed your choices down to two cars: Vehicle A costs $20,000, and Vehicle B costs $30,000. Let's also say that you'll be using your new car 100% for your business. (Although this is unlikely for most providers, I'm using it for this example since it will maximize your tax deduction.). If you spend the extra $10,000 on the higher-priced vehicle, you'll be entitled to claim an additional $10,000 deduction against your business income, although it will take a few years to claim the full amount. However, this extra $10,000 deduction won't translate into anything like $10,000 in lower taxes!

Your tax savings will depend on your family's tax bracket, which is based on your federal and state income tax rate plus the 15.3% Social Security tax on your business profit. But under any scenario, your tax bracket almost certainly won't exceed 50%. This means that even under the very best circumstances, the most you could possibly save on the extra $10,000 you have spent would be 50%. So the most you could reduce your taxes for the more expensive vehicle is $5,000.

So by buying that car, you have simply spent $5,000 more, rather than getting any additional savings. The bottom line is: *You can never save money by spending more, even if the expense is 100% tax-deductible.*

If you need to buy a bigger, more expensive vehicle because of a valid business need, then do so. However, don't decide what kind of vehicle to buy based on the tax consequences. (In fact, don't buy anything based on the tax consequences!) Instead, look for the vehicle that will meet your needs at the lowest cost. Never spend any more money than you need on a vehicle.

How to Pay for Your Next Vehicle

Most people don't pay cash when they buy a vehicle. They put some money down and borrow the rest of the cost, usually for three to five years. Taking out a vehicle loan is the only way that most people can afford to buy a car or van. In our survey, only 18% of the respondents said they were planning to make a down payment of at least 75% of the cost of their next vehicle.

However, as I explained in chapter 3, I don't believe that you should borrow money to buy a car. Paying interest on something that loses value over time, like a car, is not a good use of your financial resources—it's like slowly pouring money down the drain. Here's an example of what I mean:

Let's say you buy a vehicle for $20,000, putting $4,000 down and financing the remaining $16,000 over four years at 7% interest. Your monthly payment would be $383.14, and to pay off the loan over the four years you'd have to pay $18,390 + $4,000 = $22,390. The additional $2,390 that you've paid is 15% of the amount you borrowed. That's a lot of extra money. If you hadn't financed your car, you could have put that $2,390 into a tax-deferred investment for your retirement.

(You may hope to avoid paying this much interest by qualifying for a loan with 0% interest or a very low interest rate. However, if you take out a low-interest-rate loan, be sure to carefully check the fine print in your loan contract, since there may be hidden fees and penalties. For example, if you don't make a payment on time, you'll probably be charged a very high penalty.)

Set up a Vehicle Replacement Fund

To save money so that you will be able to pay cash for your next vehicle, you will need to build up a vehicle replacement fund first. If you can't save enough to pay the entire amount with cash, save as much as you can so that you will be able to borrow as little as possible. Let's look at the above example again, and this time see how a replacement fund could make a difference.

Instead of buying the vehicle right now and borrowing $16,000, you decide to wait six months. In the meantime, you put your $4,000 down payment into a money market account that pays 5% interest. Every month, you add $383 to that account, the same amount that you would have been paying anyway each month for your vehicle loan. At the end of six months, you would have $6,423 in the account:

Down payment	$4,000
Interest: 5% over 6 months, compounded monthly	$125
Monthly payments ($383 x 6)	$2,298
Total saved	$6,423

At that point, you could buy a used car for $6,423, and pay cash for it. However, let's say that you need a van to transport the children around, so you need more money than this. What would it take to pay cash for a larger used vehicle? After starting out like this, you'd just continue this savings plan for four years—the same time it would have taken to pay off the loan you originally intended to get. Every month you'd continue to put aside $383 into your money market account. (Although for this longer time period, you might choose another short-term savings option that would earn more interest; see chapter 2.)

Remember, this plan isn't "costing" you anything, since you'd have been paying this much every month anyway under your original plan. At the end of the four years, you'll have $25,190 in your account, including $2,806 in interest earned on your savings. You have now made the same monthly payments over the same time period as you would have done for the loan. However, you now have about $5,000 more, which will allow you to get a more reliable, safer used vehicle than the one you would have gotten with the loan! The only difference is that you were patient and waited for four years. Table 4 breaks this down by year, and you can see how your car replacement fund will add up as you go along.

Table 4. Vehicle replacement fund

	Starting balance	Contribute $383 per month	Interest earned	Ending balance
Year 1	$4,000	$4,596	$312	$8,908
Year 2	$8,908	$4,596	$563	$14,067
Year 3	$14,067	$4,596	$827	$19,490
Year 4	$19,490	$4,596	$1,104	$25,190

After saving for four years, you'll be able to pay cash for your next car with the savings you have accumulated. However, don't stop contributing to your car replacement fund at that point—now that you have made it a habit, just continue your monthly deposits. This will allow you to pay cash for a new car in another four years—or to wait a bit longer, and continue accumulating more money. If you get into the habit of doing this, you'll never have to borrow money to buy a car again.

Also, if you choose to keep your next car for longer than four years, as I recommend, you could significantly lower your monthly deposit to your car fund. For example, if you decided to keep your new car for 7 years, instead of 4, you'd only have to save $250 a month at 5% interest to pay cash for a new $25,000 car in 7 years. (And you could put away even less than that if you had some seed money, like the $4,000 that you started with above.)

Yes, I know that although this sounds so simple, it really isn't! Many people won't be able to pay cash for their next vehicle even if they start a car replacement fund today. However, I urge you to get a car replacement fund started as soon as you can, in order to reduce to the bare minimum amount you'll have to borrow for your next car. Try to keep your replacement fund going continuously from this point forward so that each time you buy a car you'll be able to borrow less, until you reach the ultimate goal of paying cash.

Note: Bear in mind that the numbers shown above are just an example to show you how this process works. The interest rates on car loans and savings accounts vary, and the best savings account rate that you can get may be lower or higher than the 5% assumed here. A different interest rate will change the amount you'd need to save each month to reach $25,000 after 4 or 7 years.

• •

How to Cope with High Gas Prices

The high price of gasoline isn't likely to abate for the foreseeable future. Here are some tips that can help you improve your gas mileage and save on vehicle expenses.

- Don't buy premium gas. Your vehicle doesn't need premium-grade gas, and regular is cheaper.

- Keep up with all the scheduled maintenance on your vehicle. Check your tire pressure, and tune up your engine on a regular basis.

- Reduce your use of gas by consolidating your short trips into fewer, longer trips.

- When you're waiting in your car, don't leave your engine idling—turn it off. Don't let the engine run to warm it up before driving in cold weather.

- Observe the posted speed limits (speeding can significantly lower your mileage per gallon).

- Remove any extra weight that you may be carrying around in the back seat or trunk of your vehicle.

- Close your windows when driving.

- Slow down when driving in residential areas to avoid unnecessary accelerating and braking.

- The next time you choose a vehicle, buy only what you need, not what you think you can afford. Consider buying a smaller or more fuel-efficient vehicle.

• •

What Are the Insurance Costs?

Before you lease a new car or buy a new or used vehicle, discuss the costs of each choice you're considering with your insurance agent. Weighing the insurance implications of your options before you make a final choice can save you a lot of money in the long run.

When you buy a newer vehicle, your insurance costs are likely to go up. Here are some ways that you might offset that increase:

- Raise your vehicle insurance deductible to $1,000; this should significantly reduce the cost of your insurance. Put the amount you save on each insurance bill into a savings account. Within a few years, you should have $1,000—enough cash to cover your higher deductible in the case of an accident.

- Combine as many of your insurance policies as you can under one insurance company. Having multiple policies with one company may qualify you for discounts and lower rates.

CHAPTER SEVEN

Getting a Business Grant or Loan

Chapter Summary

This chapter begins by examining how to get a grant for your business and the tax consequences of receiving income from a grant. The chapter then describes your options for obtaining a family child care business loan and how to maximize the likelihood that your loan application will be approved.

Grants and loans are both ways that you can get money to start or improve your business; the difference between them is that you never have to repay a **grant**. Therefore, if you need some money to start a child care business, buy new equipment for your business, or remodel your home for child care, it would be better to get the money for these large expenses through a grant rather than a loan. Since you won't have to repay the grant money, this option will allow you to keep more of your business profit.

However, you can't rely on getting a grant for the funding you need—you may not be able to obtain a grant when you need it, since there are far fewer agencies that offer grants than there are lenders who offer loans. Therefore, this chapter will also explain the best places to get a loan for your business and the steps you can take to educate your lender so that your loan application will be received favorably. (As discussed in chapter 3, your chances of being approved, and the interest rate you'll be charged, will also be strongly influenced by your credit history—refer to that chapter for more information.)

Getting a Grant

Government programs that focus on family child care providers are the most likely source of grants for your business. These programs are usually administered by local child care resource and referral agencies (CCR&Rs). Some of these programs only offer grants for specific needs, such as starting a new family child care business, adding certain services that are needed locally (such as odd-hour care or special-needs care), or making health or safety improvements. To find out if any grants are available in your area, contact your local CCR&R, your family child care association, or your licensor.

Some providers have tried to obtain a grant directly from the federal Small Business Administration (a state agency that helps small businesses), a private foundation, or an employer. But as a rule, these efforts aren't successful, since most other organizations that offer grants don't give money to businesses—they only give grants to nonprofit organizations. By default, a family child care business is classified as a sole proprietorship (a business operated by a self-employed person). Although it's possible to change your business to a nonprofit tax-exempt organization to attract private funding, it's extremely difficult to obtain nonprofit status.

If you're thinking of applying for a grant from an organization that isn't focused on grants for family child care, I suggest that you first ask if the organization has ever given a grant to an individual family child care provider before. If not, the organization is very unlikely to do so in the future.

The Tax Consequences of a Grant

As a rule, any money that you receive from a grant is considered to be taxable income. The only exception would be a grant that you receive based on low-income status, if the grant provider explicitly states that this money isn't taxable income. Since this situation is quite rare, you should assume that any grant you receive will be taxable income. If you spend the grant money on expenses that are fully deductible for your business, there will be no tax consequences, since your deductions for those expenses will fully offset your grant income.

However, what if you use the grant money to buy items that are also used by your family? To see how this works, let's say you get a $250 grant. Here are two possible scenarios:

- You use the grant to pay for items that are fully deductible—such as child development classes or small toys that are only used in your business. In this case, you'll be able to deduct the entire $250 you spent as a business expense. As a result, you won't owe any additional taxes that year because of your grant income.

- You use the grant to pay for deductible items that are used by both the children in your program and your own children. In this case, there will be a small increase in the taxes you will owe, since you'll only be able to deduct the business-use percentage of your expenses. If your business-use percentage is 40%, you'll only be able to deduct $100 ($250 x 40% = $100). Therefore, you'll still owe taxes on $150 of your grant income. Depending on your tax bracket, these extra taxes might amount to about $45 to $60.

In the above scenarios we are considering items that you can deduct fully in the year that you buy them. However, if you use the grant money to buy an item that must be depreciated over several years—such as a fence or a home improvement—then you won't be able to deduct as much; therefore, the tax consequences of your additional income will be much greater. To see how this works, let's say that you receive a $1,000 grant—here are some of the different ways you might spend it:

- You use the grant to pay for a fence that is used only for your business, such as a barrier around your play area. In this case, your deduction each year would be quite small. Since you'd be required to depreciate the fence over 15 years, your annual deduction would be about $1,000 ÷ 15 years = $67. Therefore, in the year you get the grant you'd have to pay taxes on $1,000 − $67 = $933 in extra income, which would probably amount to about $280 to $375. However, over the next 14 years, the $67 annual tax deduction would slightly reduce your taxes (by about $20 to $25 a year).

- You use the grant to pay for a fence that is also used for personal purposes, such as a property line fence. In this case, your annual depreciation deduction would be lower, since you'd only be able to depreciate the business-use portion of the expense. So compared to the previous example, you'd have to pay more income taxes for your grant income in the first year, and you'd save less in taxes over the remaining 14 years that you're depreciating the fence.

- You use the grant to pay for a home improvement that is only used for your business. In this case, your deduction would be even lower than for a fence, since home improvements must be depreciated over 39 years, rather than 15 years. Since this home improvement is used 100% for your business, your annual depreciation deduction would be about $1,000 ÷ 39 years = $26. Therefore, the first year you'd have to pay taxes on $1,000 − $26 = $974 in extra income, which would probably amount to about $292 to $390. In the remaining 38 years, your taxes are unlikely to be reduced by more than $10.

- You use the grant to pay for a home improvement that is used for both business and personal purposes. In this case, your deduction would be the lowest of all, and you'd have only a very small depreciation deduction. In the first year, you'd have to pay taxes on virtually all of the additional $1,000 in taxable income, and in the remaining years you'd be unlikely to see a tax savings of more than a few dollars a year.

Also bear in mind that if you use grant money to buy an item that must be depreciated over multiple years, you will only be allowed to take the annual depreciation deduction for that item as long as you remain in business. So if you use the grant income to buy a fence or a home improvement and go out of business shortly after that, then you won't be able to claim any of the remaining depreciation deductions in subsequent years.

I don't believe that you should refuse to accept a grant just because it may increase your taxes—raising the quality of your program should be your primary concern. However, it's important to understand that when you receive a grant, you may end up having to pay some extra income taxes that year. As long as you recognize that, go ahead and enjoy the improvements you can make with the grant money. For more information about the tax consequences of grants, see the *Family Child Care Record-Keeping Guide*, 7th Edition.

Getting a Business Loan

If you can't find an agency that will give you a grant to start or improve your program, you may have to take out a loan to get the money you need. In comparison to grants, there are many organizations—both businesses and nonprofit groups—that might be willing to give you a loan. Where should you look first? Although your first response may be to visit your bank or credit union, that may not be the best place to look for a family child care loan. There are many other organizations that may be more willing to lend you money:

- Some states have loan programs that focus specifically on family child care providers. To find out if there is such a program in your area, visit the Web site for the National Children's Facilities Network, www.ncfn.org/ff.htm. If one of these loan programs is available in your area, I recommend that you go there first.

- Ask your local child care resource and referral agency if there are any public or private loans or grants that you could apply for. For additional grant and loan resources, contact the National Association for Child Care Resource and Referral Agencies (www. ChildCareAware.org; 800-424-2246).

- If you have a permanent life insurance policy—also known as whole life, universal life, variable insurance, or cash-value insurance—you may be able to borrow against your policy at a very low interest rate. Your policy may also allow you to pay back only the annual interest, rather than making monthly payments. Just bear in mind that taking out a loan on the value of your policy will reduce your life insurance benefits if you die before paying back the principal that you borrowed.

- Contact one of the "microenterprise" loan programs that assist small businesses such as family child care providers. For more information, see the large directory of organizations that offer small loans to child care providers at nccic.acf.hhs.gov/poptopics/micro-directory.html.

- The federal Small Business Administration (SBA) sponsors Office of Small Business Development Centers (SBDC) that may be able to help you find a loan by referring you to local resources. Find out more at www.sba.gov.

- Contact a women's business center in your area; some of them offer loans to family child care providers. To locate a center in your area, visit the Office of Women's Business Ownership (OWBO) sponsored by the SBA. Find out more at www.sba.gov.

- Ask your relatives or friends for a loan. To avoid the possibility of falling apart over a financial dispute, be sure to put your loan agreement in writing. Your loan agreement should include a specific repayment plan—when you'll begin paying the loan back, how much you'll pay each month, and how much interest (if any) you'll pay over the term of the loan.

Notice that credit cards aren't mentioned here. I strongly recommend that you don't use your credit card to "loan yourself" any money. Credit card interest is far higher than any of the loan options identified above, and can even exceed 20%. You should only use your credit cards for purchases that you'll be able to pay in full at the end of the month, as described in chapter 3.

The process of applying for a loan will involve a lot of paperwork and stress, and the documents you will be signing are important. (For example, you may be required to put up your home as collateral.) Be sure to read the fine print on all documents closely before you sign. Don't sign anything until you have asked enough questions to make sure that you fully understand and are willing to agree to those terms.

• •

Get a Copy of Your Credit Report

When you apply for a loan, the lender will review your credit report and credit score to determine if you're a reasonable credit risk. Therefore, before you look for a loan, it's a good idea to order a copy of your credit report and check it for accuracy. You're entitled to receive one free credit report each year from each of the three major credit rating companies—Experian, Equifax, and TransUnion. For more information about your credit report and how to order a copy, see chapter 3.

• •

Educate Your Lender about Your Business

Paradoxically, if you have been conscientiously recording and claiming all your business expenses, you may find that these diligent efforts will work against you when you apply for a loan. The problem arises because banks and other lenders will usually look at your business profit to determine whether you can afford to pay back the money you want to borrow. A loan officer will typically just look at the net profit shown at the end of your **Schedule C**, and if this number isn't large enough, she may deny your loan application without inquiring further.

The solution to this dilemma isn't adjusting your return to show a bigger business profit by claiming fewer business expenses. I strongly recommend that you not alter your tax return in the hope of making it easier to get a loan. Giving up your rightful tax deductions will hurt you financially.

Instead, there are two steps you can take to educate a loan officer about your true financial situation and increase your chances of being approved for a loan—adjusting your **Schedule C** income to show the bank what it really wants to know and showing the bank a cash flow statement for your business.

Adjust Your Schedule C Income

What your lender really wants to know is whether you have the financial ability to pay off the loan that you are applying for. However, the guidelines that most lenders use to evaluate your creditworthiness were developed for other kinds of businesses, and your loan officer may not understand how your family child care is different unless you explain it to her. Specifically, she will probably assume that the net profit on your **Schedule C** reveals how well your business is doing. However, as a family child care provider, the net profit on this line is *not* an accurate reflection of your business finances.

Here's why. There are significant expenses shown on your **Schedule C** that shouldn't be counted in determining your ability to pay off a loan. That's because these expenses either aren't directly caused by your business or they aren't "real" expenses for your business that year. The IRS allows family child care providers to claim certain expenses that other kinds of small businesses aren't allowed to claim. Although these expenses reduce your net profit, they don't represent an additional cost to you this year.

To more accurately reflect the financial status of your business from a lender's standpoint, you will need to calculate your profit for the most recent tax year without these expenses. Start by writing down the business profit shown at the bottom of your **Schedule C**, and then take a look at the following lines on your tax return:

- Record the amount shown on the line "Expenses for Business Use of Your Home" on **Schedule C**. This amount is the total of the expenses you have claimed on **Form 8829**— your mortgage interest, property taxes, homeowners insurance, home depreciation, home repairs, and utilities. As a rule, these expenses don't cost you any more just because you're in business, so they shouldn't be included in evaluating your business profit.

- Record the amount shown on the line "Depreciation and Section 179 Expense Deduction" on **Schedule C**. This amount is the total of the depreciation deductions you have claimed on **Form 4562**. Most of these deductions don't represent money that you have actually spent in the current year, such as your ongoing depreciation for furniture, appliances, play equipment, computers, and possibly your vehicle (depending on the method you use to deduct vehicle expenses).

    This total will also include any Section 179 expenses that you have claimed that year. Although you did pay for these expenses this year, you should argue that these expenses shouldn't be considered in evaluating your ability to pay off a loan, since they won't be repeated.

- Add up the amounts, if any, shown in Part IV of **Form 8829**. This will give you the total of any home expenses (including home depreciation) that you have carried over from a previous year in which you couldn't claim these deductions because your business showed a loss. These deductions shouldn't be counted against your current year's business profit, since you didn't pay for them this year.

Add up the above amounts, and then add that total to the net profit shown on your **Schedule C**. This will increase your net profit. For example, let's say that the net profit shown on your **Schedule C** is $20,000. Your home expenses from **Form 8829** and your depreciation expenses from **Form 4562** add up to $5,000. You didn't have any carryover home expenses entered in Part IV of **Form 8829** that year. You add this $5,000 to your net profit to get a revised business profit of $25,000.

On the same page, describe where each number in this calculation is located on your tax return, and explain that the revised profit number more accurately represents the profit from your business and therefore how much money you'll have to pay off the loan. Attach this page to your **Schedule C** when you submit your tax return to the lender.

• •

The Tax Consequences of a Loan

Any income that you receive from a loan is not taxable income. Any interest that you pay on a loan that you have used for business purposes is deductible on your **Schedule C**. If the loan was for something that is used only in your business (such as children's furniture), then you can deduct all of the loan interest. If the item is used for both personal and business purposes (new windows, kitchen remodel, finishing the basement) then only the business-use percentage of the loan interest will be deductible. For more information, see the *Family Child Care Tax Workbook and Organizer*.

• •

Show Your Cash Flow Statement

The second way of educating your loan officer about your true financial picture is to show her a cash flow statement for your business. Lenders usually evaluate businesses in terms of their monthly profit and loss—how much money comes in and goes out each month. They want to know if you'll have enough money left over after paying your other expenses to make the monthly loan payment.

The best way to show this information is to give the loan officer a cash flow statement. To learn how to prepare a cash flow projection for a start-up or ongoing family child care business, see the *Family Child Care Business Planning Guide*. If you have prepared a cash flow projection for your business, then give your lender a copy of that document. The loan officer may also ask for more information, such as your actual cash flow numbers for the recent past, or she may ask you to add your living expenses and any other personal income to your statement.

Your cash flow projection will show exactly how much income and expenses you expect to have each month, and how much will be left over at the end of the month. To support your loan application, your projection will need to show that you will have enough left over every month to be able to afford the loan payments you're applying for.

If you're starting up a new family child care business, you won't have a **Schedule C** to show the loan officer. In this case, follow the instructions in the *Business Planning Guide* for preparing a business plan, first-year budget, and first-year cash flow projection, and show her those documents. Your business plan can make a big difference at this point by showing how carefully you have planned your new business.

If you're trying to borrow a significant amount of money, or if getting the loan will determine whether or not you can open your business, you may want to get some assistance from an accountant to ensure that your financial picture is presented in a professional way that will inspire the lender's confidence.

• •

More Tips to Help You Get a Bank Loan

If you're planning to apply for a bank loan, I suggest that you download a copy of the Enterprise Foundation's "Financing Family Child Care" booklet, which has helpful advice about getting a loan from a bank. You can download your free copy from www.enterprisecommunity.org/resources/publications_catalog/#child. (This is the same PDF booklet that includes tips for choosing a credit counseling service—see chapter 3.)

• •

Don't Give Up

You may need to be persistent and spend some time educating your lender about your business. For example, if the loan officer won't accept the higher net profit that you have calculated, don't give up—ask to speak to her supervisor. If you have been in business for a long time, use this as another reason why you would be a good loan risk.

If you are turned down for a loan anyway, try another lender. If you're a reasonably good financial risk, eventually you're likely to find a lender who is willing to learn about your business. If that doesn't work, as a last resort you could ask another family member to cosign a loan for your business. However, I have spoken with a number of providers who simply refused to give up—and whose persistence was eventually rewarded with the loan they were seeking.

CHAPTER EIGHT

Hiring Employees

Chapter Summary
This chapter examines what you need to know if you are considering hiring an employee. It explains how to evaluate the financial consequences of taking on an employee and explains the tax and insurance implications that this decision raises. It also provides a checklist of the steps that you will need to complete before and after hiring an employee.

It should be so simple—you just want to hire someone to help you care for the children on a part-time or full-time basis. However, in reality, hiring an employee is a complex decision that raises some serious tax, insurance, and legal issues that you ignore at your own peril. Before you decide to hire an employee, you need to understand what this choice will mean and carefully consider all the costs and benefits involved.

Who Is an "Employee"?
To make sure that you stay in compliance with the law, you need to understand the legal definition of an employee according to the IRS and other regulatory agencies. With very few exceptions, anyone you pay to help you care for the children in your home is an employee, not an independent contractor. There are only two exceptions:

- A person who presents a special event in your home—such as putting on a puppet show or providing dance or swimming lessons—is not your employee.

- A person who is in the business of providing substitute care for child care providers is not your employee, as long as she is operating as a self-employed business. She should have a registered business name and a taxpayer identification number, provide services for several providers, and have her own contract. If she doesn't meet these criteria, then you must treat her as your employee.

Many providers make the mistake of assuming that they can treat a helper as an independent contractor if they pay her less than $600 in a year. This is not true. Anyone you pay is an employee, regardless of how little you pay her.

If you hire your spouse or your child to help you care for the children, you must also treat him as an employee. (However, if you hire your child and she is younger than age 18, you won't have to withhold Social Security taxes or pay federal unemployment taxes for her.) For more information about the difference between an employee and an independent contractor and the tax rules for family members whom you employ in your business, see the latest edition of the *Tax Workbook and Organizer*.

Requirements for Employers

For many family child care providers, the complex regulations and tax forms that employers must file are the biggest obstacles to hiring an employee. To meet the federal and state rules, you will need to do several things:

- Obtain an employer identification number. You can do this by filing **Form SS-4** or filling out the appropriate form at www.irs.gov.

- Confirm that the employee is eligible to work in this country by filing **Form I-9**.

- Determine if you must withhold federal income taxes from the employee's paycheck by asking the employee to fill out **Form W-4**.

- Withhold Social Security and Medicare taxes from your employee's paycheck.

- Make regular deposits for the employee's Social Security and Medicare taxes—either quarterly with **Form 941** or annually with **Form 944**.

- Pay the employee's federal unemployment taxes each year by filing **Form 940**.

- Report the Social Security and Medicare taxes that you paid each year by filing **Form W-2** and **Form W-3**.

- File any other forms required for state unemployment taxes and other state taxes.

- Determine if you have to pay the federal minimum wage of $6.55 per hour or a higher state minimum wage. (The federal minimum wage will rise to $7.25 in July 2009.) If you have just one employee who isn't a family member, you won't have to pay the federal minimum wage.

- If required by your state, buy workers' compensation insurance. (And I recommend that you buy this insurance even if it isn't required.)

When faced with all of these forms and taxes, many providers feel like throwing up their hands in frustration! (Sorry, it always pains me to list these requirements.) However, you don't have to do it all yourself. You can get help from a tax preparer. Also, there are payroll services that can do most, if not all, of this work for you—you can find these services by looking under "bookkeeping services" in a phone or online directory. If you prefer to do it yourself, see the latest edition of the *Tax Workbook and Organizer* for an explanation of how to fill out all the federal forms.

• •

Employee Benefits

In addition to paying all the required federal and state taxes, you may want to provide your employees with benefits such as paid vacations and holidays or other time off. You could also offer medical benefits, an employee retirement plan (described in chapter 16), or training to improve the employee's child care skills. However, you aren't required to offer any of these benefits.

• •

Compare the Costs and Benefits

Most providers consider hiring an employee primarily in order to expand their program and increase their profits by caring for more children. So what you really want to know is "Will hiring an employee to help me care for more children actually increase my profit?" The answer to this question will depend on how many more children you will be able to enroll after hiring the employee.

The worksheet in table 5 will allow you to weigh the costs involved in hiring an employee against the added income that you expect to earn by caring for more children. (Both online and downloadable versions of this worksheet are also posted at www.redleafpress.org. Type "money management" in the search box and follow the links.) The first column in table 5 shows the numbers for Lainie, a provider who is considering hiring an employee to help her care for two more children. You can enter your own numbers in the second column.

In Lainie's case, caring for two additional full-time children wouldn't offset the cost of hiring a full-time employee—she would actually lose $49 per week. However, if Lainie were able to enroll three more children, it would be worthwhile to hire a full-time helper. In that scenario, Lainie would make $81 more per week ($140 x 3 children = $420; $420 + $27 – $57 = $390; $390 – $309 = $81).

Bear in mind that table 5 is just an example—your new employee's hourly wage, her hours worked, your other employee costs, your weekly fee per child, and your Food Program income per child will probably all be different than shown there. Also consider the following assumptions that are made in this worksheet:

- This worksheet may not include all your employee costs; for example, you may be required to pay state employment taxes or buy workers' compensation insurance for your new employee.

- This worksheet doesn't include any increased business expenses (such as toys and supplies) that may be involved in caring for more children.

Table 5. Worksheet: Weekly expenses involved in hiring an employee

Cost of employee	Lainie's Numbers	Your Numbers
Employee's hourly wage	$6.55	_____
Hours per week that the new employee will work	x 40	_____
Employee's weekly salary	= $262	_____
Payroll taxes (8.45% for Social Security, federal unemployment taxes)	+ $22	_____
State employment taxes	+ $0	_____
Workers' compensation insurance	+ $0	_____
Other employee costs (training, supplies, food, other benefits, etc.)	+ $25	_____
Total weekly employee costs	= $309	_____
Additional income		
Number of new children enrolled	2	_____
Weekly fee per child	x $140	_____
Weekly fee income for new children	= $280	_____
Weekly Food Program income for new children*	+ $18	_____
Weekly food expenses for new children**	– $38	_____
Total additional weekly income	= $260	_____
Net weekly income or loss ($260 – $309)	– $49	_____

* Lainie's number on this line is based on the 2007–2008 Tier II daily rate of $1.82 per day per child ($1.82 x 5 days x 2 children = $18). For your numbers, multiply by the current Food Program rate.

** I'm simplifying this example by assuming that Lainie's food costs will be the same as the 2008 IRS standard meal allowance. For your numbers, enter your actual weekly food expenses for the new children on this line.

This worksheet also assumes that you will be able to quickly enroll the additional children that you wish to add to your program. If you aren't able to maintain your new enrollment target, you won't make the weekly profit calculated above, and you may lose money every week. If you aren't sure you'll be able to fill the additional slots in your program, deciding to hire an employee can be a difficult dilemma. As one provider put it:

> I've determined that the only way to really make any money in this business is to be a large licensed provider. However, for me that presents an insurmountable dilemma. In order to become such a provider, I would have to hire, or be ready to hire, a full-time assistant. But paying someone for 40 hours a week before all my slots are full is financially impossible since I am a small family child care provider—Catch-22. Therefore, I will continue to make very little money.

Even if you are able to fill all your slots right away when you hire an employee, you still need to have a plan for the possibility that one or more of the children may leave your program. If that happens, your choices will be to continue paying your employee her full salary, cut back her hours, or lay her off. Since you will have less income at that point, if you keep your employee on, her salary and expenses may be coming from your pocket until you can fill the slots again.

• •

Insurance Issues for Employees

Hiring an employee exposes you to the risk that she'll become injured on the job or be accused of child abuse. Your state may require you to buy workers' compensation insurance that will cover your employee in the case of an on-the-job injury. However, I recommend that you buy workers' compensation insurance even if it isn't required. You will also need to add business liability insurance coverage for your employee to protect yourself from liability for her actions while in your employ. (The cost of adding an employee to your liability insurance policy should be minor.)

• •

Is it worth going to all this trouble to hire an employee? Yes, if you are able to enroll enough new children. As a rule, the financial gains from hiring an employee will usually be minimal or nonexistent unless you are able to enroll at least three more children. However, this decision may not be primarily about the money. It may be worth it for you to hire an employee simply in order to improve the quality of your program, give a helping hand to someone who needs a job, enjoy the company of another adult during the day, or be able to spend more time with your own family.

Checklist for Hiring an Employee

Even after sorting through all the tax, financial, and insurance issues discussed above, you may still have concluded that you would like to hire an employee, either for financial or nonfinancial reasons. In that case, there are several steps that you'll need to complete before and after hiring your employee. Here's a checklist to help guide you through these steps:

Before You Hire

- Contact your licensor and ask if there are any state regulations about the qualifications of the workers you hire. Your state may also require that you do a background check.

- Check with your state department of labor for its guidelines on hiring and firing employees (for example, to avoid illegal discrimination).

- Find out if your home is subject to any deed restrictions, homeowners association covenants, or zoning laws that might restrict your right to hire employees.

- Carefully screen your potential employees. Do a criminal background check and a credit check, confirm their references from previous employers and coworkers, and confirm their educational credentials.

- Write an employee manual that explains your state's law about corporal punishment and its mandated reporting law for child abuse. To set the standards for your employees, you may want to refer to the Code of Ethical Conduct adopted by the National Association for Family Child Care (www.nafcc.org). This code covers a child care provider's ethical responsibilities to children, families, and employees.

After You Hire

- Instruct your employees in your health, safety, and emergency procedures. For example, make sure that they understand who is authorized to pick up each child and any special custody arrangements for the children in your care.

- Give your employees training (or send them to workshops) on child abuse and neglect, CPR, child development, and appropriate ways to discipline children.

- Closely supervise your employees, and conduct regular reviews of their performance. In your reviews, be sure to discuss personal and work stress and provide stress management suggestions. This will help keep the children in your program from being negatively influenced by their caregivers' stress.

- Discuss your privacy and confidentiality policies for communicating with the parents of the children.

- If one of your employees uses her car in your business, you can buy "hired and non-owned liability" coverage that will protect you against lawsuits if she causes an accident and injures someone. If an employee will be driving your car for your business, make sure that she is covered by your vehicle insurance policy.

For further information about the legal and insurance issues related to hiring employees, see the *Family Child Care Legal and Insurance Guide*.

CHAPTER NINE

Moving Your Business Out of Your Home

Chapter Summary
This chapter examines the issues involved in moving your business away from your home, including the advantages and the disadvantages of such a move. It explains the financial consequences and other issues that you should weigh in making this decision.

Some states will allow you to operate a family child care business out of a building that you don't live in. If you have been considering such a move, this chapter will explain the effects of this choice on your business and personal life to help you decide. This kind of move will be a major change, and before you take it, you should carefully consider its pros and cons and how it will affect your business, financially and in other ways. Moving your business is likely to have both regulatory and financial consequences:

- **Regulatory consequences**: If you want to move your business away from your home, some states will require you to establish a child care center—and the regulations for child care centers and family child care businesses may be quite different. Check with your child care licensor to find out your state's rules for operating a child care business from another building, what regulations would apply if you move, and how this change would affect your business.

- **Financial consequences**: Moving your business away from your home will have both advantages and disadvantages financially. The move might allow you to earn more money by caring for more children. However, your expenses will be higher, and you'll lose the home deductions that you can claim for running your business in your home.

The Pros and Cons of Moving Your Business

Let's start by looking at the overall advantages and disadvantages of moving your child care business away from your home. Depending on your situation, the advantages of such a move might include the following:

- Moving your business out of your home will give your family more privacy and unrestricted access to all the rooms in your home. They won't have to live with any of the clutter generated by the toys and paperwork for your business.

- The new location might have more space that will allow you to care for more children, and therefore generate more income.

- The new location might be more suitable for child care, or it might be in a better neighborhood where the parents are willing to pay more.

- If you buy the new building and its property values rise, the equity that you build could help you meet your long-term goal of saving for retirement.

The disadvantages might include:

- Since you will be living in your home and operating your business in another building, you'll be paying expenses for two buildings. This will increase the cost of expenses such as rent or mortgage, repairs, insurance, property taxes, and utilities. Although the operating costs of the new building will be fully deductible, the resulting reduction in your taxes won't completely offset the additional expenses.

- The higher expenses described above will reduce the amount of cash you have available for personal use.

- If you buy the new building and its value rises, when you sell it you'll need to pay capital gains taxes on the difference between what you paid for it and what you sold it for. (For more information, see the latest edition of the *Tax Workbook and Organizer*.)

The Financial Consequences

In most cases, the financial pros and cons listed above will roughly balance each other out. Therefore, as a rule it will only make financial sense to move your business out of your home if this will allow you to make significantly more money by caring for more children. To see why, let's look at the financial trade-offs in more detail. Table 6 shows a simplified comparison based on a fairly typical family child care scenario. (This comparison is simplified because this kind of move involves very complex tax and financial issues, as we'll see.)

As table 6 shows, if you move your business into a new building, you'll be able to deduct all of your expenses for that building, which will reduce your net profit on your **Schedule C**, and thus the income and Social Security taxes that you will owe.

However, your tax bill isn't the most important consideration in this comparison. The number that you should pay the most attention to is how much cash you'll have on hand at the end of the year. In the example shown in table 6, paying $10,000 in additional expenses for the new building would reduce your cash on hand at the end of the year by $8,200 ($11,500 – $3,300). If you were in the 30% tax bracket, you'd need to earn roughly $12,000 more in the new building to replace this lost income: $12,000 x 30% taxes = $3,600; $12,000 – $3,600 = $8,400.

Table 6. Comparison of annual expenses for moving your business out of your home

Your home		Another building	
Income	$35,000	Income	$35,000
Home expenses ($10,000 x 40% Time-Space percentage): mortgage, taxes, insurance, utilities, repairs	– $4,000	Building expenses (fully deductible): mortgage, taxes, insurance, utilities, repairs	– $10,000
Other business expenses	– $6,000	Other business expenses	– $6,000
Net profit	$25,000	*Net profit*	$19,000
Business taxes (30%)	– $7,500	Business taxes (30%)	– $5,700
Nondeductible home expenses	– $6,000	Nondeductible home expenses	– $10,000
Cash on hand at year-end ($25,000 – $7,500 – $6,000)	$11,500	*Cash on hand at year-end* ($19,000 – $5,700 – $10,000)	$3,300

If your child care rate was $120 per week, and you worked 50 weeks a year, you could earn this additional $12,000 by caring for two more full-time children. But remember that the additional income from these two children won't raise your overall cash on hand at the end of the year; it will only raise your profit to the amount you were making at home.

Making Your Own Comparison

The numbers used in the above scenario may be very different from your own situation—the intention here is just to show you how to weigh the major financial issues involved in your decision. In looking at your own numbers, bear in mind the following assumptions I've made in table 6 that you may want to adjust:

- I've kept the home expenses the same for both scenarios. In your own comparison, consider whether any of your home expenses, such as utilities or insurance, will change when you move your business out of your home.

- I've kept the business income the same for both scenarios. In your own comparison, enter the annual income that you expect to make in the new location for the second scenario.

- I haven't taken into account any equity you might earn by buying the new property. Over time you'd hope that your equity will increase, resulting in a substantial profit when you sell the building. However, owning property isn't a sure thing financially—you'll need to pay property taxes and maintenance expenses over the years you own the building, and the profit you'll ultimately make will depend on the real estate market at the time. Therefore, I wouldn't include this equity in your own comparison either.

Also bear in mind that in a real-life scenario, you will need to analyze the financial trade-offs of your decision in far more detail than shown above. If you're serious about evaluating the financial consequences of moving your business, you should consult a tax preparer and an accountant, and ask them to prepare a more detailed version of this table that reflects your unique circumstances.

Although it's important to know what you're getting into financially, you may choose to operate your business in another building despite a lower cash flow if your family's privacy is the most important issue for you. However, I do suggest that you weigh all the financial consequences so that you will be able make an informed decision about what will be best for you and your family.

• •

You Won't Be Able to Deduct Your Commuting Miles
Also bear in mind that once you move your business, you won't be able to count your mileage between your home and the new building as a business trip, since these trips will be considered commuting. (You will still be able to deduct the mileage for any trips that you take from one business location to another.)

• •

Checklist of Other Issues

If you're considering moving your business to a new location, here are some additional issues that you should check out first:

- As mentioned above, ask your child care licensor about your state's regulations. Many states require a family child care provider to operate her business in her primary residence. Some states (such as California) may allow you to move your business to another building only if you meet the more stringent rules that apply to child care centers.

- If you're thinking of buying the new building, find out what the property taxes will be. Since you won't be living in that building, you'll probably have to pay the commercial tax rate, which is generally higher than the tax rate you're paying for your home.

- Contact your county zoning office and check any homeowners association bylaws for your new property to make sure that you will be allowed to run a child care business in that location.

- Talk to your homeowners and business liability insurance agent to determine the cost of insurance for the new building.

- Talk to your car insurance agent and make sure that you will still be covered for any accidents while using your vehicle for business purposes.

- Ask your tax preparer to "run the numbers" for the new building and advise you about the tax implications of making a move.

CHAPTER TEN

Handling Major Transitions

Chapter Summary
This chapter describes some of the major tax and financial issues that you
should be aware of if you're in the process of getting a divorce or closing your
family child care business.

This chapter will examine some of the short-term and long-term consequences of two major
kinds of life transitions—getting a divorce and closing your child care business. You may
find yourself in one of these situations unexpectedly, and in the midst of the stress it may
be easy to overlook some of the implications of the decisions you are making. This chapter isn't meant to be a comprehensive guide to all the tax or financial issues that might be
involved in these situations (especially in a divorce). Nevertheless, this discussion can help
ensure that you have considered the major issues that apply specifically to family child care
providers so that you can take appropriate steps to protect your financial interests.

Getting a Divorce

Each year there are over one million divorces in the United States. There is a 43% chance
that a first marriage will end in separation or divorce within 15 years. Although it may be
uncomfortable to contemplate the possibility of a divorce, every married provider should
understand how a divorce might affect her business and her financial future.

All divorces involve a distribution of assets—and typically, the result of this distribution
will be a significant decline in the woman's economic status. If there is a large difference in
earning capacity between you and your spouse, one of you may be required to pay alimony
or spousal support to the other. If dependent children are involved, then child support payments may also be required.

Dividing up the couple's property, pensions, retirement accounts, and other assets can be
very complicated, and the rules vary from state to state. As a result, a divorce may have a
significant impact on your taxes and your overall financial situation, including your long-
term financial plans. For example:

- You will now be responsible for paying all of your taxes. This may mean that you will have to start paying quarterly estimated taxes after the divorce.

- If you will be keeping the home in which you have been doing child care, you should be aware of the tax consequences of selling that home, and take this future liability into account in the divorce settlement.

- A divorce may have major implications for your retirement plans, especially if you have been expecting to rely on income from your spouse's Social Security account, pension, or retirement plan.

I will discuss each of these issues in more detail below. The division of assets in a divorce may also raise other financial issues, including health insurance, life insurance, and the savings for your children's college education. Because of the complexities of these issues, if you're getting divorced, I strongly recommend that you seek professional help from a lawyer, a tax professional, and a financial planner. You will want to assemble a team that can represent your interests in the divorce settlement and make sure that you get a fair deal.

And of course, these are just the financial effects of a divorce—the emotional issues involved can be extremely painful and may take years to heal. There are resources that can help you through this process, such as www.womansdivorce.com, a site that is dedicated to "helping women survive divorce and rebuild their lives."

Paying Your Taxes

Your filing status for your tax return is based on your marital status as of December 31 of a given year. This means that you'll file your first return as a single person or a head of household for the tax year in which your divorce becomes final. You'll be able to claim all your normal business deductions as before; they won't be affected by your filing status. You will also continue to fill out all your business tax forms as you did before.

However, the picture gets more complicated if you were previously filing jointly and your spouse was withholding enough money from his paycheck to cover your estimated tax payments. If you didn't pay any estimated taxes in the final year of your marriage because you were relying on your spouse's withholding, you'll owe a penalty for any estimated taxes you should have paid that year because you'll now be filing your taxes under your own name, and your soon-to-be ex-spouse's withholding was done under his name.

In your divorce settlement, ask your spouse to cover your tax bill—federal and state income taxes, Social Security taxes, and any penalty you might owe—for the final year of your marriage.

If your husband is self-employed and has been paying all of the family's taxes through his own estimated tax payments, then you can claim part of his estimated tax payments on your tax return for the final year of your marriage. For more information, see IRS **Publication 504 Divorced or Separated Individuals**.

Examine Your Business and Personal Finances

Without your spouse's income, it may be more difficult for you to make ends meet by relying solely on your child care business. Therefore, a divorce (or the death of your spouse) is a good time to reassess your business and consider ways to increase your income such as those discussed in chapter 4. You may also want to start budgeting your income and expenses to help you manage your new financial reality.

If you have not already done so, consider preparing a business plan and budget, as described in *Family Child Care Business Planning Guide*.

Selling Your Home

If you're being awarded your home in the divorce settlement, then you should be aware of—and ask your husband to share—the tax liability that you'll face when you sell the home. (This liability will be explained further in the next section about closing your business.)

To explain how this works, let's say that you have been married and doing child care in your home for 10 years, and now you are getting divorced. Over those 10 years, you have been entitled to claim a business deduction for the depreciation of your home; for our example, let's say that the amount you were entitled to claim was $1,000 per year, for a total deduction of $10,000 over the 10 years. (It doesn't matter whether you actually claimed this deduction or not, just that you were entitled to do so.)

When you sell your home, you will owe taxes on this $10,000, plus additional depreciation if you continue operating your business in the home (but that future depreciation won't be an issue in your divorce). While you were married, your spouse shared the tax benefit of the $10,000 depreciation deduction during those years; therefore, it makes sense to ask him to pay at least half of your future tax liability for those years.

Depending on your tax bracket at the time you sell, the tax you will owe on the $10,000 could be as high as 25%. If you're in the maximum 25% bracket at that time, you'll owe $2,500 in taxes on the $10,000 of depreciation that you were entitled to take while you were married.

You'll want to bring this tax liability to the attention of your divorce lawyer so that she can take it into account in negotiating your settlement. If you want to keep the house for the foreseeable future, your tax preparer can help you estimate the likely amount of this future tax bill. You should expect your spouse to pay at least half of that amount as part of the divorce settlement. It will be much better to get the money now, so that you can invest it and let it grow, than to simply have an agreement that he will share the cost whenever the house is sold.

For more information about the tax consequences of selling your home, see the latest edition of the *Tax Workbook and Organizer*.

Social Security Retirement Benefits

While you're married, you have the option of taking joint Social Security retirement benefits equal to half the benefits earned by your spouse rather than any individual benefits you have earned (I'll explain this more fully in chapter 11). If you have been counting on receiving half of your spouse's Social Security retirement benefits, it's important to understand the rules about how a divorce will affect your eligibility for joint benefits.

In order to receive benefits based on your husband's Social Security account, you must have been married to him for 10 years. If you were married that long and your spouse is entitled to receive Social Security benefits, then you will be eligible to start collecting half of what he is entitled to receive once you reach age 62.

If you have any questions, visit www.socialsecurity.gov or contact the Social Security Administration at 800-772-1213.

• •

Social Security Survivor's Benefits

If your former spouse dies after you divorce him, you will still be entitled to receive survivor's Social Security benefits as early as age 60. If you have legal custody of a child under age 19, your child may also be entitled to survivor's benefits.

• •

Pensions and Retirement Accounts

Most family child care providers are counting on income from their husband's pension or retirement plan to help support them in retirement. A divorce will jeopardize this future income and can unexpectedly throw a monkey wrench into your retirement plans. If your husband qualifies for an employer's pension plan, be sure to include this asset in negotiating your divorce settlement.

Your settlement should also consider any IRAs that your husband has contributed to. If you are granted some of your husband's retirement savings, make sure that the funds are transferred to you as part of the divorce settlement to avoid paying the 10% early withdrawal penalty on the IRA. If the money from your husband's retirement plan is deposited directly into an IRA that you have set up, you won't have to pay any income taxes on this money until you begin withdrawing it for your retirement.

However, if you will need to use some of the money from your husband's IRA before you retire, then don't have that portion of the money deposited directly into another IRA. Otherwise, you will have to pay the 10% penalty when you want to withdraw the money. Just bear in mind that you'll need to pay income tax on any money from your husband's IRA that isn't deposited directly into your IRA.

Other Issues

During the divorce, your husband may contend that the value of your child care business should be considered in dividing your joint assets. As a rule, this argument has no merit. Your business is based on your personal services. If you tried to sell your business, it would be worth very little to anyone else unless you continued to run the business and provide child care. There may be some value in your equipment, toys, children's furniture, and other supplies, but nothing more than that.

In dividing your assets, your business profit (after expenses) should simply be compared to what your husband earns. The fact that you are self-employed and operating your own business doesn't add any value that should be considered as part of the divorce settlement.

Closing Your Business

Family child care businesses have a high turnover rate—and even if you do stay in business for many years, the day will eventually come when you'll realize that it's time to close up shop. When you close your business, there are three issues that may affect your taxes, either that year or in the future:

- The way you dispose of your toys and equipment may increase or decrease your taxes in the year you close your business.

- You may have to calculate your Time-Space percentage differently for your final year in business.

- In the year you close your business, you may have to pay back some of the business depreciation that you have claimed, which will increase your taxes that year.

- You'll have to pay more taxes in the year that you sell a home that you have used for your child care business.

I'll discuss each of these issues below, along with some comments about filing the tax return for your last year in business and the final steps you'll need to take when you close your business. For more information about all of these topics, talk to your tax preparer or consult the latest edition of the *Tax Workbook and Organizer*.

Dispose of Your Toys and Equipment

By the time you close your business, you may have rooms filled with toys, games, clothing, arts and craft supplies, sports gear, and playground equipment. There are several ways that you can dispose of these items, and each option will have different tax consequences. Typically, providers dispose of these items by one of these means:

- selling them at a garage sale
- selling them or giving them away to another provider
- donating them to charity
- throwing them away

Selling your toys and equipment at a garage sale may have some consequences, either positive or negative, for your taxes. If you buy a toy for $50, deduct it fully as a business expense, and later sell it at a garage sale for $5, you will have made a $5 gain on that item, which is taxable income.

If you sell a swing set that you have used partly for your business and were depreciating as a business expense, you may have a loss on that item that will reduce your taxable income. You will need to take these tax consequence into account whether you sell the items before or after you go out of business.

Giving your toys and equipment to a new provider would be a nice gesture of support. Just bear in mind that you won't be able to claim a charitable contribution for any donations to other providers, since you aren't giving the items to a registered charity.

If you donate your toys and equipment to a charity, you may (or may not) be able to claim a charitable deduction for your contribution. If you have already fully deducted the item as a business expense, then you won't be entitled to a charitable deduction for it. If you're still depreciating it, then you may be able to claim a charitable deduction. Here are some examples:

- You buy a stroller for $200, and fully deduct its cost as a business expense. Some years later, when the stroller is worth $50, you donate it to a charity. In this case, you won't be able to claim a charitable contribution, since you have already deducted the full cost of $200.

- You buy the stroller for the same price but start depreciating it rather than deducting the full $200. When you donate the stroller some years later, you still haven't taken the full amount of depreciation you were entitled to claim. In this case, it's possible that you'd be entitled to take a charitable contribution, although it wouldn't be the full value of $50. I won't go into all the details here, since this is a complicated area—for more information, refer to the *Tax Workbook and Organizer*.

In donating items to charity, also bear in mind that small items that are donated to a charity must be in good condition in order to qualify as charitable donations for tax purposes.

If you decide to just throw away all your toys and equipment, there will be no tax consequence, other than (possibly) the lost opportunity to reduce your taxes that year by claiming a charitable deduction or showing a loss for any items that haven't been fully depreciated.

Calculate Your Final Time-Space Percentage

If you close your business at the end of the calendar year, you'll calculate your Time-Space percentage for that year as usual. However, if you close your business at any other time during the year, you'll have to calculate your Time-Space percentage a bit differently, since your business wasn't open for the entire year. Here's how to do this:

1. Calculate your Time percent: Add up all the hours that you worked in your home in your last year of business, and divide this by the total number of hours in the months (or days) that you were in business that year.

2. Calculate your Space percent: Do this in the same way you've done it in previous years.

3. Calculate your Time-Space percentage: Multiply your Time percent by your Space percent.

The only difference is in step 1, where you will have to calculate your Time percent differently than usual—so let's look at an example of that calculation.

Let's say that you close your business on August 31, and you worked 60 hours a week through your closing date. This means that you worked 2,100 hours during that year (60 hours x 35 weeks). Since there are 168 hours in a week (24 x 7), the total number of hours between January and August 31 is 5,880 (168 x 35). Therefore, your Time percent for your final year is 36% (2,100 ÷ 5,880 = 36%). Multiply 36% by your Space percent to get your Time-Space percentage for your final year in business.

Use the adjusted Time-Space percentage that you calculate as described above for only the expenses that you incur in your final year of business (in the above example, that would be from January through August). For more information, see the *Record-Keeping Guide*, 7th Edition.

Claim Your Final Depreciation Deductions

It's quite likely that when you close your business, you'll still be depreciating certain business items such as your furniture, appliances, computers, and home or yard improvements. Once you close your business, you won't be entitled to claim any of the remaining depreciation for these items; you will simply stop claiming these depreciation deductions on your future tax returns. However, in this final year, your depreciation for some items will need to be calculated differently; for more information, consult a tax preparer or the *Tax Workbook and Organizer*.

As a rule, you won't have to repay any of the business depreciation that you have already claimed, but there is one exception—any items that you have deducted using the Section 179 rule. If you used this rule to claim the full cost of any depreciable items in the year you bought them and you go out of business before the depreciation period for that item expires, then you will have to pay back some of the deduction that you originally claimed. Consult a tax preparer to find out if this applies to you.

When You Sell Your Home

When you sell a home that you've used for your business—whether it's immediately after you close your business or many years later—you'll have to pay taxes on any depreciation that you were entitled to claim on your home after May 1997. You'll have to pay these taxes in the year you sell your home, regardless of whether or not you actually claimed this depreciation deduction while you were in business.

In other words, if you were entitled to take depreciation of $1,000 a year and were in business for six years, then when you sell your home you will owe taxes on $6,000. (The previous section on handling a divorce has a more detailed example of this calculation.)

The good news is that you'll probably be able to avoid paying any capital gains taxes on the profits you make when you sell your home. If you're married and filing jointly, the IRS currently allows you to avoid paying a capital gains tax on your first $500,000 in profit, as long as you owned and lived in the home for at least 2 of the 5 years before you sold it. If you're single, the profit limit is $250,000.

If your home has been extensively customized for your business—for example, with a downstairs play area, a separate entrance, or an extensive outdoor play area—these alterations could affect the amount that potential buyers might be willing to pay when you put your home on the market. A potential buyer who has children of her own, or who would like to do child care herself, may be willing to pay extra for your home because of these features. However, other buyers may not be interested in these features and may feel that they reduce the value of your home.

• •

Selling Your Business

It's unlikely that you'll be able to sell your business, because its value is based on the personal services that you have been providing. Parents choose to join your program because they want you to care for their children. Once you leave, your clients will move on to another child care provider. Therefore, your business and business name will usually have little, if any, value that you can sell.

• •

File Your Final Tax Return

The last year that you are in business, simply file your business tax forms as usual—**Schedule C**, **Form 8829**, and so on. If you have any employees that year, also file your quarterly payroll tax forms and your end-of-year federal and state (if applicable) tax forms, as usual. You don't need to do anything to inform the IRS that you're going out of business. In subsequent years, you just won't file your business tax forms anymore.

Take the Final Steps

There are three key steps that you will need to take when you close out your business—giving notice to parents, notifying regulatory and professional agencies, and updating your insurance coverage.

• **Give notice to parents**. In closing your business, plan ahead when and how to tell your child care parents that you will be closing. If you give the parents too much advance notice, they may start looking for another program and leave sooner than you would like.

Since you're about to close your business, it will probably be difficult to fill these spaces. On the other hand, you don't want to give the parents such short notice that they'll have difficulty making other arrangements in time.

I recommend that you notify the parents that you'll be closing a month or two in advance. Although you'll want to tell each parent in person (or at least on the phone, if that isn't possible), be sure to follow up by giving them a written notice of your closing date, to avoid any confusion later: "The last day I will be able to provide care for your child will be _____."

- **Notify regulatory agencies and professional organizations**. Once you have gone out of business, notify your licensor or state regulatory department, your local child care resource and referral agency, your Food Program sponsor, and your local family child care association, and ask them to update their records.

- **Update your insurance coverage**. Finally, contact your insurance agent. Cancel your business insurance coverage—your policies for business property, business liability, and the business use of your vehicle—and ask if you are entitled to a refund for any future coverage that you have already paid for. Bear in mind that once you stop using your home and car for business, you may have a wider variety of insurance companies to choose from—so this may be a good time to shop around and see if you can get a better deal.

PART III

Prepare for Retirement

CHAPTER ELEVEN

Social Security and Pensions

Chapter Summary

This chapter discusses the income that you'll be entitled to receive after
you retire from employer pensions and Social Security. It explains Social
Security retirement benefits in depth, including how to maximize your
retirement benefits under that program. It also looks at two other sources
of retirement income, earned income and investment income.

The first two parts of this book have primarily focused on short-term money management
skills—how to increase your income and savings, reduce your debt and expenses, and handle the financial aspects of specific decisions and issues. In this chapter, we'll begin to look
at long-term financial planning—preparing for retirement. In this context, "long term" may
mean 20, 30, or 40 years into the future. (Yes, this chapter is for you, even if your retirement
is still 40 years away—just keep reading, and you'll see how important it is to be thinking
that far ahead.)

Retirement can mean different things to different people; for the purposes of this book,
I'm defining it as the time when you have achieved enough financial freedom to do whatever you want. Doing whatever you want may mean not working at all, working part-time,
or starting a new career without the pressure of having to support yourself on the income
you're earning.

This chapter will help you identify the base income that you will be entitled to receive
from pensions and Social Security after you retire. Chapter 12 will explain how to calculate the remaining amount you'll need to retire and how much you should be saving now
to accumulate that nest egg. Chapter 13 will explain how you can start working toward that
goal now, regardless of your current income. Chapters 14 through 16 will explain how to
invest your retirement savings wisely.

You may be able to do all your retirement planning yourself, following the guidelines
given in chapters 14 through 16—or you may prefer to seek professional help. If you wish
to work with a financial advisor, chapter 17 will show you how to pursue that option.

Most people can potentially draw upon four possible sources of income to support themselves in retirement:

- pension income
- Social Security income
- earned income (if you continue working after retirement)
- investment income (from the retirement savings you have invested)

(If you're married, you may also be able to rely on your husband's income from one or more of these four sources—"Marry a rich man!" was one provider's financial advice.)

This chapter will outline the role of each of these four income sources, while primarily focusing on Social Security. We'll start here because the first step in retirement planning is figuring out how much income you'll receive from pensions and Social Security when you retire. For most people, retirement income from these sources will be easier to estimate than income from investments, which is dependent on future returns in the stock market.

Pensions

Traditional pensions provide a guaranteed income in retirement in return for a certain number of years of service. Pensions aren't a source of significant retirement income for most family child care providers. In our survey, only 27% reported that their family had qualified for an employer pension—and this number is only likely to go down, since each year fewer and fewer U.S. workers are covered by employer pensions.

Employers are increasingly turning over the responsibility for retirement planning to their employees by offering **401(k) and 403(b) retirement plans** instead of pensions. These retirement plans don't provide a guaranteed retirement income as a traditional pension does. Instead, they are investment plans that provide the same tax savings as an IRA plan. (If you aren't sure what this means, read on—I'll be explaining investments and IRAs in chapters 14 through 16).

In our survey, 9% of the providers said that their family expected to receive less than $10,000 a year in pension income, 9% said their family would receive between $10,000 and $25,000 a year, and only 8% expected to receive more than $25,000 a year. Most of this pension income was generated by the provider's spouse. You'll only be able to earn pension benefits yourself if you are employed by someone else at some point in your life—typically, before starting your child care business.

If either you or your spouse expects to receive any income from a traditional pension in retirement, contact the pension plan administrator and ask for an estimate of how much income you'll be receiving. (You'll need this estimate to complete the worksheet in the next chapter, which will help you figure out if your pension income plus your Social Security benefits will provide enough money for you to retire on.)

Social Security

As a self-employed person, you need to understand how the Social Security program works and what you need to do to maximize your benefits. As a rule, Social Security is designed to replace only about 40% of your current earnings. (Only low-income providers are likely to receive more than 40% of their current income in Social Security retirement benefits.)

The retirement benefits that you'll receive will be based on the Social Security taxes that have been paid into your account on your behalf. Self-employed people, such as family child care providers, pay a Social Security tax of 15.3% of their business profit when they file their federal tax return each year. An employed person, on the other hand, only pays half of this amount (usually by payroll deduction)—the person's employer contributes the other half.

To qualify for Social Security benefits, you must pay Social Security taxes for at least 10 years. (The years don't have to be consecutive—you just need to accumulate 10 years over all your working years.) If you were employed or had another business before starting your family child care business, you may already have partially or fully qualified for Social Security. (I'll explain how to find out if you have qualified later in this chapter.)

Once you qualify, you can retire as early as age 62 and receive a reduced retirement benefit, or you can wait until your full retirement age and receive full benefits. You also have the option of waiting a few years longer and receiving even higher benefits.

Social Security also offers other kinds of benefits that you can qualify for if you have paid Social Security taxes for at least 5 of the last 10 years before you claim the benefits. These include disability benefits that will replace part of your income if you become unable to work before full retirement age, and survivor benefits that will be paid to your spouse and children after you die.

• •

Will Social Security Still Be Around When I Retire?

Since there's been a lot of public debate about the future of the Social Security program, some people wonder whether it will even be around to pay them when they are ready to retire. The answer is that if you have qualified for Social Security retirement benefits, you're certain to receive at least some income from Social Security, even if the payments are lower than the current levels. Therefore, it's important to do whatever you can to maximize your Social Security benefits.

• •

Make Sure You Qualify for Social Security

Many family child care providers work with their tax preparers to keep their net profit, and therefore their taxes, as low as possible each year. In this way, some providers are able to show little or no profit over several years. However, if you have a loss or a business profit of less than $400, you won't have the option of paying Social Security taxes that year, so that year won't count toward the 10 years required to qualify for Social Security benefits.

In our survey, 16% of the providers didn't achieve $400 in profit in the previous year—5% showed a loss, 8% showed zero profit, and another 3% showed a profit of less than $400. If any of these providers were still working toward qualifying for Social Security, that year wouldn't count toward that goal.

Qualifying for Social Security is an important strategy for increasing your retirement income, since if you fail to qualify, you won't get any individual benefits when you retire. To illustrate this, let's look at an example.

Chantelle and her friend Tori both decide to open a family child care business in 1996. Both are single, and neither of them has had any previous work experience. Tori operates her business for nine years, from 1996 to 2005, earning $10,000 in profit each year. In 2005 she closes her business and retires at age 66. Chantelle, who is one year younger, operates her business for one more year, from 1996 to 2006, also earning $10,000 in profit each year and closes her business to retire at age 66.

The only difference between the two friends' circumstances is that Chantelle has worked one more year, for a total of 10 years, which allows her to qualify for Social Security. As a result, by 2010, Chantelle will be receiving about $278 a month from Social Security, while Tori will get nothing. In 2010 dollars, Chantelle's benefits will add up to $3,336 per year, or a total of $66,720 over 20 years of retirement.

• •

How to Pay Your Social Security Taxes

As a self-employed person, you don't need to send the IRS a separate check to pay your Social Security taxes each year. You'll pay these taxes by filing **Form 1040SE Self-Employment Tax** with your annual tax return. You'll calculate your Social Security taxes on that form, and then add them to your other taxes on **Form 1040**. If you don't pay close attention to your tax forms, you may not even realize that you're paying Social Security taxes, especially if you hire a tax preparer to fill out your tax return for you.

• •

It's not unusual to show an occasional loss on your tax return, and anyone can have a bad year now and then. However, if you haven't yet qualified for Social Security, don't intentionally reduce your profit below $400, if you can avoid it. Instead, try to show a profit of at least $400 each year until you qualify. In some years, this may mean not taking all the deductions that you're entitled to claim.

This advice may seem strange coming from me, especially if you've been faithfully following my recommendations and claiming all your allowable deductions over the years. In general, it's still true that you should take all the deductions that you can—but making sure that you qualify for Social Security is an important exception to this rule.

Once you have qualified for Social Security by meeting the 10-year requirement, you will no longer need to keep showing a profit of at least $400 each year. At that point, resume taking all your deductions to reduce your business profit as much as possible. It's true that showing a higher profit will increase your Social Security benefits down the road. However, the impact of an extra few thousand dollars in profit will not materially affect your Social Security benefits—so you're better off claiming all your deductions, showing a lower profit, and investing the money you've saved on taxes in a tax-deferred retirement account.

The bottom line is *make sure that you qualify for Social Security benefits*. Find out how many years you still need, if any, to qualify, and set a goal of showing a profit of at least $400 for that number of years, even if you have to reduce your deductions to do so. Once you have qualified for Social Security, resume claiming all your allowable deductions.

• •

If You're Married

If you're married, you have another option for receiving Social Security benefits. If your spouse has qualified for significantly higher Social Security benefits than you have, you can choose to claim half of his benefits instead of any individual benefits you have earned.

So if your spouse will be receiving $1,000 per month from Social Security, you'd be entitled to claim benefits of $500 per month, even if you haven't qualified by meeting the 10-year rule. However, if your individual benefits will amount to more than half of your spouse's benefits, then it's probably better for you and your spouse to both claim your individual benefits. (If you're wondering how your joint benefits would be affected by a divorce, see chapter 10.)

• •

Your Social Security Statement

Each year, a few months before your birthday, you'll get a statement from the Social Security program showing all the details of your status in the program. (These statements are sent to all taxpayers age 25 and older.) It's worthwhile to review this document closely, since it explains how the Social Security system works and provides a lot of information that will be helpful in planning your retirement:

• The statement shows your earnings history by year and tells you whether you have worked enough years to qualify for benefits.

- If you have qualified for benefits, the statement will show your expected retirement benefits under the current laws (estimated by projecting your previous year's income), including how much you can expect to receive if you retire at age 62, at your full retirement age, and at age 70.

- The statement shows the age at which you can retire with full benefits, based on the current laws.

- The statement explains the assumptions used to project your estimated benefits so that you can adjust the estimates if you know that those assumptions aren't realistic.

- The statement shows how much you can expect to receive if you become disabled before your full retirement age.

- The statement shows the amount of survivor benefits that your family can expect to receive if you die.

When you get your statement each year, review the earnings history on page 3, and confirm that the totals shown there are accurate and complete. The income shown for each year should be the same as the net business profit you reported on **Schedule C** that year, plus any other gross income you earned that year, as shown on line 7 of **Form 1040**.

Don't just assume that the Social Security program must have the correct numbers. For example, if you were employed before opening your business, your employer would have been responsible for reporting the Social Security taxes that she paid on your account. If she failed to do that in one or more years, some of your income may be missing from your Social Security record.

If you see any errors in the income recorded, be sure to correct them, since any missing income will probably lower the retirement benefits you are entitled to receive. You don't want to wait and discover the error when you're about to retire—waiting longer can make it more difficult to find the documentation you'll need to correct the mistake.

If you believe there's an error in the earnings history shown on your statement, or if you have any questions about your statement, call the Social Security program right away at 800-772-1213 to get it straightened out. (If this phone number changes, the new number will be listed on your statement.)

• •

If You Can't Find Your Social Security Statement

If you don't have a copy of your latest Social Security statement, you can request a copy online at the Social Security Web site (www.socialsecurity.gov). Or you can call the Social Security office at 800-772-1213. In either case, ask for Social Security **Form SSA-7004**.

• •

As explained above, the estimated retirement income shown on your Social Security state-ment is calculated by simply projecting your previous year's income. However, if that isn't a realistic assumption, or if you just want to estimate how a change in your income would affect your Social Security benefits, you can use a benefit estimator to calculate the benefits yourself. Also, if you're near retirement age, you may want to get a better idea of the actual payment you'll be receiving after annual cost-of-living increases. Next, I'll explain how to make these kinds of adjustments to your Social Security income.

Using a Benefit Estimator

Social Security retirement benefits are calculated using a complex formula that's based on how much you pay into the program over a 35-year period. The Social Security Web site (www.socialsecurity.gov) has some online calculators that you can use to estimate your retirement income based on your own assumptions.

You might also be able to get a rough idea of what you can expect to receive (in 2008 dollars) by looking at table 7. This table assumes that you have no other work experience and that you operated your business for thirty years. (For estimating purposes, I'm using the years 1978 to 2007.)

Table 7. Social Security retirement benefit estimator

Annual business profit for 30 years (1978–2007)	Social Security income (2008 dollars)	
	Monthly	Annual
$10,000	$815	$9,780
$20,000	$1,223	$14,676
$30,000	$1,582	$18,984

Table 7 shows that if you earned an average profit of $10,000 per year from 1978 to 2007 and then retired at your full retirement age, you could expect to receive the equivalent of $815 per month ($9,780 a year) in 2008 dollars.

The numbers shown above will rise each year, since Social Security benefits are increased annually to keep up with inflation. For more recent numbers, use the calculators at the Social Security Web site (www.socialsecurity.gov) to estimate your benefits.

Adjusting for Inflation

Social Security benefits are increased each year based on the current inflation rate (in 2007 and 2008, inflation has been running around 3% to 4%). The estimated benefits shown on your Social Security statement are given in today's dollars. However, you can add the effects of inflation to those estimates—here's how to do that.

Let's say that you plan to retire in five years at age 62. Your latest Social Security statement says that you'll receive $1,000 a month at that age, and you'd like to add the effects of inflation to that number. If you assume that there will be a 4% annual inflation rate for the next five years, you could project your future benefit as follows:

Year 1: $1,000 x 1.04 = $1,040
Year 2: $1,040 x 1.04 = $1,082
Year 3: $1,082 x 1.04 = $1,125
Year 4: $1,125 x 1.04 = $1,170
Year 5: $1,170 x 1.04 = $1,217

So if Social Security benefits increase by 4% each year, as assumed here, when you retire in five years you can expect to receive about $1,217 per month. Of course, in that time your living expenses are also likely to increase by an average of 4% per year, so in terms of buying power you'll still be getting the equivalent of today's $1,000.

When Should You Retire?

The Social Security rules currently allow people to start receiving some retirement benefits as early as age 62. Full retirement age begins at age 66, depending on your year of birth (see your Social Security statement). If you retire at age 62, your monthly benefits will be lower throughout your retirement, but you'll receive them for more years.

If you wait until full retirement age, you'll receive more each month, but for fewer years. You can even wait until age 70 to start drawing Social Security benefits, in which case your monthly payments will be even higher, but you'll receive them for fewer years.

So when should you retire? There's no simple answer to this question. If you're in poor health or under financial stress, you might choose to retire and start receiving benefits as soon as possible. If you're able to continue working, you might want to try to wait longer.

Since this is an important decision and each person's situation is different, I strongly recommend that you consult a financial planner or a Social Security representative at least a few years before you're thinking of retiring to help decide what will work best for you.

• •

Continuing to Work after Taking Social Security

If you start taking Social Security benefits before your full retirement age and continue to work, your benefits will be reduced if your earnings are above a certain amount. Since these limits are subject to change, if you intend to work while collecting Social Security, check to see how much you can earn without a reduction in your benefits. Once you have reached your full retirement age, you can earn as much money as you want and not have it affect your benefits. (To find out your full retirement age, check your Social Security statement.)

• •

Earned Income

After adding up the retirement income that your family can expect to receive from pensions and Social Security, you'll probably discover that there's still a gap—the total so far just isn't enough to live on after you retire. (I'll show you how to do this exercise in the next chapter.) To fill that gap, you may have considered another source of retirement income—continuing to work after retirement.

Many retired Americans don't have enough money to stop working altogether, so they continue working. That's why we see so many seniors working at information desks, fast food restaurants, and department stores. For many seniors, working part-time is necessary to make ends meet.

Family child care is hard work, harder than many other jobs that seniors are hired to do. Nevertheless, some of the providers in our survey planned to continue caring for children as long as they were physically able to do so. But one of them added, "With each passing year I realize that this is an exceptionally physically demanding job, and I wonder how many more years I can handle it." Simply put, your health may not allow you to work as long as you want to.

The providers in our survey identified health problems as a major concern. They worried that health problems might prevent either the provider or her spouse from working as long as she wished, leading to a loss of that person's income and any employer benefits associated with it. So bear in mind that although you might plan to work after retirement, you may not be able to do so.

Investment Income

The idea of relying on income from our own investments in retirement is a relatively new concept. Traditionally, the combination of income from a pension, Social Security, and possibly part-time work was enough to allow most people to maintain a reasonable standard of living during retirement. No more. Because of longer life expectancies and a decline in traditional pensions, most of us will need to rely on our own investments to make retirement possible.

Since we're living longer, on average we can expect to spend about 25% of our years in retirement. This means that we'll need to invest our savings wisely to provide a stream of income that won't outlive us. Our investment income will also need to grow fast enough to outpace the annual increases in the cost of living caused by inflation.

We can't do that much to increase the income that we'll receive from Social Security (other than qualifying for benefits and checking that all our income is reported). However, investing our retirement savings is completely up to us. For many readers, this topic may be the most important part of this book—so I'll spend the next five chapters discussing it in detail.

CHAPTER TWELVE

How Much Should You Be Saving?

Chapter Summary
This chapter will help you figure out how much money you'll need to save to support yourself in retirement. You'll complete a worksheet that will give you a rough estimate of your retirement savings target and will show how much you need to save each month to meet that goal.

Now that you have found out how much retirement income you'll be getting from pensions and Social Security, the next question is, how much should you be saving for retirement? Although this question sounds simple, the answer is complex. For one thing, to figure out how much you should be saving now, you need to know how much you'll need to have when you retire.

Some experts say that most people will need about 70% to 80% of their working income in retirement to maintain their standard of living. However, no one really knows if that guideline is correct. My father was a financial planner for many years before he retired. Once he retired, I asked him what the magic number was—70%, 80%? He said, "100%"!

The best answer is probably that you'll need as much money as you have saved. Your lifestyle in retirement will be based on the amount of money you have to spend. If you haven't saved very much, you'll somehow manage to live on less. If you have saved more, you'll have a broader range of options after you retire.

So a better question might be, "How much will I need to live a retirement lifestyle that I'd be content with?" Start by thinking about how much money you'll need to live on after retirement. If you plan to stay where you are and not change your lifestyle very much, then your current spending may be a good guideline. If you'd like to expand your horizons by traveling more, going out to eat more often, and taking longer vacations, then you'll need more money than you have today. Also bear in mind that although some expenses (such as clothing and mortgage payments) may go down after you retire, others (such as medical care and entertainment) may go up.

Another way to look at what you should be saving for retirement is to follow a simple formula that my father shared with me: save 10% of your take-home pay (or business profit) for retirement, give away 10% to charity, and live on the remaining 80%. The key to this program is learning to live on less than you make. If you can learn that lesson while you're working, it will be much easier to manage your money in retirement. (One provider in our survey echoed my father's advice, "Always save at least 10% of what you make!")

• •

Women Need More Retirement Savings than Men

It's especially important for women to save their money and plan for retirement, for several reasons:

- On average, women live longer than men.

- On average, women earn less than men, so their Social Security benefits are lower too.

- Women may have more medical expenses after retirement because they live longer than men.

- Women may face a significant reduction of their standard of living if they become divorced or their husband dies first.

For more information about these issues and what you can do about them, visit the Web site for the Women's Institute for a Secure Retirement, www.wiserwomen.org.

• •

It will be a lot easier to estimate your retirement living expenses if you're already approaching retirement age. However, you can't wait for that kind of certainty—as we'll see later in this chapter, it's important to start saving as soon as possible.

If you have no idea what your retirement expenses will be, start with the adjusted gross income from your latest **Form 1040**—the number on the bottom line on the first page. (This number will include the net business profit you reported on **Schedule C** plus any gross wages earned by you—or your spouse, if you're filing jointly.) Multiply the number on this line by 75%. The result is as good a guess as any about how much money you'll need to live on in retirement.

Estimate How Much You Need to Save

Starting with this 75% of your adjusted gross income, complete the worksheet in table 8 to get a rough estimate of how much income you'll need for retirement and how much you should be saving to reach that goal. (This worksheet uses 2008 dollars; you'll need to recalculate your retirement needs annually as your income and financial circumstances change.)

Table 8. Worksheet: How much should you be saving for retirement?

	Sally's Numbers	Your Numbers
1. How much annual income will you want in retirement? *Begin by entering 75% of your current income before taxes; you can always re-estimate later using a higher or lower number.*	$21,000 *(75% of $28,000)*	$_____
2a. Subtract the annual retirement income you expect to receive from Social Security. Enter the estimated annual retirement benefit from your Social Security statement, or your adjustment of that number. *You can also use a rough estimate of your retirement benefits—if your current gross income is less than $25,000, enter $8,000; between $25,000 and $40,000, enter $12,000; more than $40,000, enter $14,500. (Bear in mind that these are greatly simplified estimates.)*	– $12,000	– $_____
2b. Subtract any annual retirement income you expect to receive from a traditional employer pension. (Enter only income from a traditional pension, not income from an employer's 401(k) or 403(b) plan.)	– $0	– $_____
2c. Subtract any annual retirement income you expect to receive from earned income after you retire.	– $0	– $_____
2d. Subtract any other annual retirement income you expect to receive.	– $0	– $_____
3. Subtract lines 2a through 2d from line 1. This is the amount of annual retirement income that you need to make up.	$9,000	$_____

4. To determine how much you'll need to save, multiply line 3 by the factor for your gender and the age you expect to retire:

Retire at	Female	Male
age 55	20.5	18.8
age 60	18.3	16.3
age 66	15.8	13.5
age 70	12.8	10.2

= $142,200 = $_____
($9,000 x 15.8)

5. If you expect to retire before age 66, you'll need to add an amount to offset your lower Social Security benefits. To do this, multiply line 2a by the factor for the age at which you expect to retire:

age 55	8.8
age 60	4.7

+ $0 + $_____

6. Subtract the income that your current savings will yield in retirement. To get this number, multiply your current savings by the factor for the number of years left before you will retire:

10 years	1.3
15 years	1.6
20 years	1.8
25 years	2.1
30 years	2.4
35 years	2.8
40 years	3.3

– $18,000 – $_____
($10,000 x 1.8)

Table 8 *(continued)*

	Sally's Numbers	Your Numbers
7. Total savings needed at retirement (line 4 + line 5 – line 6)	= $124,200 ($142,200 + $0 – $18,000)	= $_____
8. To determine how much you need to save each year, multiply line 7 by the factor for the number of years left before you will retire: 10 years 0.085 15 years 0.052 20 years 0.036 25 years 0.027 30 years 0.020 35 years 0.016 40 years 0.013	$4,471 ($124,200 x 0.036)	$_____
9. To determine the amount you need to save each month, divide the annual savings amount on line 8 by 12.	$373	$_____

Source: Based on "Get a Ballpark E$timate® of Your Retirement Needs" (www.choosetosave.org/ballpark), courtesy of the American Savings Education Council.

This worksheet assumes that you will live to age 86 (if you're female) or age 82 (if you're male). This is a reasonably conservative assumption.

This worksheet assumes a constant real rate of return of 3% after inflation. In other words, if inflation is 4%, your savings will earn 7%. This is a reasonable, if not conservative, assumption.

The right-hand column on this worksheet is blank so you can fill in your own numbers. If you're married, you and your spouse should each fill out your own worksheet and then add your totals together. On line 2a, the lower-earning spouse should enter her own Social Security benefit or 50% of her spouse's benefit, whichever is higher.

The left-hand column shows an example of how to fill out the worksheet. This example is for Sally, a provider who is single and earns a profit of $28,000 on her business each year. Sally has already saved $10,000 toward her retirement. She is now 46 years old and plans to retire in 20 years, when she reaches age 66. To determine how much savings Sally will need to retire, we'll assume that she'll begin to receive income from Social Security at age 66 and will live to age 86.

Experiment with Your Assumptions

Looking at the bottom line in the left-hand column of table 8, we can see that Sally would need to save $4,471 per year (or $373 per month) for the next twenty years to reach the retirement income goal of replacing 75% of her current income. But let's say that Sally (or you) got to that last line and exclaimed, "I can't possibly save that much!" If the number on the last line just isn't possible for you, then go back and redo the worksheet, changing some of your assumptions.

For example, could you live on 70% of your current income after retirement? Sally thinks that she could—so she does her worksheet again, this time starting with 70% of her current adjusted gross income. For this scenario, she finds that she would need to save $3,675 per year, or $306 a month.

For Sally, that's still too much. So she considers working part-time in retirement, maybe for a local Realtor or caterer, which she has always wanted to do. By playing around with her assumptions on the worksheet, Sally discovers that if she could earn just $4,000 a year after retirement, she'd only need to save $1,400 per year ($117 a month). Although this would be much more affordable, it would require Sally to keep working until she drops dead.

So as a last resort, Sally considers working five years longer. She discovers that if she waits until age 70 to retire, she will only need to be saving $2,060 per year, or $172 per month. Although this will be a stretch, she figures that it's a goal she can live with. She reviews her finances, looking for ways to reduce her spending and raise her income to make this new goal possible.

Even after experimenting with the worksheet like this, you may still find it difficult to see how you'll be able to save enough for your retirement. Some providers can draw upon other financial resources to help them meet their retirement goals: their spouse's savings, a family inheritance, or help from their parents or in-laws. Others work part-time at other jobs to earn their retirement money or switch to another career that will allow them to save more money.

Also bear in mind that this worksheet assumes you will retire completely once you reach a certain age. This probably isn't a realistic scenario—you may know many "retired" people who are still working, and this is especially likely to be true for self-employed people. A more likely scenario is that you will retire gradually, continuing to work after you start receiving Social Security benefits, whether from financial necessity, love of your work, or a desire to use your skills to help others. Some retired providers reduce their hours by caring only for children after school, running a summer day camp, or providing backup care for other providers.

Determining the amount that you need to save for retirement can be complicated. As this worksheet shows, there are many considerations that will affect the amount of retirement savings you'll need to accumulate, including your age, the rate of return on your investments, the inflation rate, when you start taking Social Security benefits, whether you keep working after that, whether you or your spouse has a pension, and your current level of retirement savings.

However, this worksheet can give you a way to experiment with the factors that you can control and to explore your options. It can give you a realistic picture of where you stand now, and reveal the choices that you may need to make. Although this may be a sobering experience, it's better to understand your situation now, when you have at least some time to prepare, than to be surprised by it later—the closer you get to retirement, the less time you will have, and the narrower your options are likely to be.

A More Aggressive Savings Goal

If you can afford it, you may wish to aim for a more aggressive savings goal to ensure that you will be well-prepared for retirement. To do that, you can use this alternate way to estimate how much money you'll need to save:

1. Figure out the annual income you want to live on in retirement. (For example, you may want to aim for 100% of your current gross adjusted income.)

2. Subtract from that number the annual income you expect to receive from Social Security and pension benefits.

3. Multiply the result by 25 to get your total savings goal at retirement.

4. Insert your new goal into line 4, and complete the worksheet.

For example, let's say that Sally would like to retire at age 66 and have income of $28,000 per year after she retires. However, in this new scenario, she worked before starting her business, so she has already saved $25,000, and she expects to have $15,000 in annual Social Security benefits.

Sally starts by subtracting her Social Security income from her desired annual income: $28,000 – $15,000 = $13,000. Then she multiplies $13,000 by 25 to get a total savings goal of $325,000. She enters that number on line 4 of the worksheet and uses lines 5–9 to figure out that she would need to be saving $10,080 per year, or $840 per month, to be able reach that more aggressive goal.

Refine Your Estimate

I have intentionally made the retirement savings worksheet in table 8 as simple as possible to make it easier for you to get started. This worksheet will give you a rough estimate of your retirement needs to use as a starting point. However, ideally you'll go on from there and do a closer analysis, either by using a more detailed worksheet or by working with a financial planner (which I'll discuss in chapter 17).

There are many Web sites that offer sophisticated retirement planning calculators that you can use to refine your savings estimate. Below are some of the sites that offer these tools—and most of these sites also provide other helpful information about retirement planning. For each site, I've given the name of the tool and described how to find it.

- www.aarp.org. Look for the "Retirement Calculator" in the Money section.

- www.fidelity.com. Look for the "Retirement Income Planner" in the Retirement Planning section.

- www.smartmoney.com. Look for the "The SmartMoney Retirement Worksheets" under Personal Finance > Retirement Planning.

- www.choosetosave.org. This site provides links to retirement calculators from several organizations; to find them, look under Calculators > Retirement Calculators.

- www.cnnmoney.com. Look for the "Retirement Planner" under Personal Finance > Calculators.

- www.hughchou.org. Look for the "Updated Retirement Calculator" under Mortgage and Other Financial Calculators > Retirement.

(The above instructions were accurate as of July 2008. If a site is redesigned after that and you can't find the calculator using these instructions, try searching the site for the name shown in quotes. Even if the tool is moved to another page, its name will probably stay the same.)

. . . .

Many Retirement Payments Are Taxable

In planning how much money you'll need to retire, be sure to take into account any income taxes that you'll need to pay on your retirement income. Retirement payments that you receive from a pension plan are taxable income. Most distributions from 401(k) and 403(b) plans are also taxable, and in many cases, even Social Security payments are taxable. Consult a tax professional to find out if your retirement income will be taxable and how much you'll need to set aside for taxes.

. . . .

You Aren't Alone

After going through this planning process, you may be wondering *(a)* how in the world you'll ever be able to meet your retirement savings goal, and *(b)* what other providers are doing to save for their retirement. We'll look at the first question in the next chapter, where we'll discuss some workable strategies for meeting your savings goal.

As for the second question, the short answer is that many providers just *aren't* saving for retirement—or at least not nearly enough. I'll show you what I mean, using the results from our survey. However, in looking at these statistics, bear in mind that our survey respondents appeared to be more financially savvy than the average provider—they had more experience than average, and virtually all of them described themselves as either "somewhat" or "very" knowledgeable about managing their money. So, if anything, the true picture is probably worse than these numbers would indicate.

Our survey asked, "How comfortable are you that you are saving enough for retirement?" Over two-thirds of our respondents (69%) said they were "not at all comfortable" with their retirement savings. Of the rest, 24% said they were "somewhat comfortable," and only 7% said they were "very comfortable."

When we asked, "How would you describe your retirement planning?" only 11% of our respondents said they had "detailed plans" for how they would save enough money for retirement. The remainder were evenly split between having "some plans" (44%) and having "no plans" (44%).

Next, we asked for more specifics—"How much do you and your spouse currently have saved for retirement (not counting a pension)?" We found that most of them had saved less than $10,000. Specifically, the responses were:

less than $10,000	55%
$10,000 to $50,000	19%
$51,000 to $100,000	13%
$101,000 to $250,000	8%
$251,000 to $500,000	3%
$501,000 to $1,000,000	1%
more than $1,000,000	< 1% (one provider)

Of course, to put the total saved so far into context, we need to consider the savings by age group, as shown in table 9. But the numbers in this table aren't any more encouraging. For example, the table shows that about one-quarter of the providers in their sixties have saved less than $10,000 for retirement, and only about half of the providers in their forties and fifties have saved any more than that amount.

Table 9. Retirement savings by age group

Amount saved	Age Group				
	20s	30s	40s	50s	60s
Less than $10,000	80%	62%	47%	46%	24%
Between $10,000 and $50,000	11%	21%	20%	19%	6%
Between $50,000 and $100,000	9%	12%	14%	12%	24%
Between $100,000 and $250,000		5%	12%	10%	24%
Between $250,000 and $500,000			6%	9%	6%
More than $500,000				3%	17%

We also asked providers if they had made any contributions to an IRA or employer's retirement plan in the previous year. More than half of the respondents said they hadn't made any such contributions. The responses to this question were as follows:

no contributions	56%
$1 to $1,000	6%
$1,000 to $2,000	7%
$2,000 to $5,000	17%
$5,000 to $10,000	9%
more than $10,000	5%

Where Do You Stand?

When you saw these numbers, you probably recognized right away that they show a pervasive problem. Regardless of age, most of the (relatively savvy) providers who responded to our survey are not saving enough money to replace anything like their current income in retirement. Family child care providers are no different from most Americans; as a culture, we tend to focus on the present and put off preparing for the future.

When it comes to retirement, knowledge is power. So regardless of how much or how little you've saved so far, by estimating how much you will need to save for retirement, you're probably already ahead of almost half of your peers—because remember: even among these experienced providers, 44% had *no* plans for retirement.

Although you now know what you need to do, you may not yet understand how to go about doing it. Where do you go from here? The next chapter will explain how to start making progress toward your retirement savings goal.

CHAPTER THIRTEEN

How You'll Reach Your Savings Goal

Chapter Summary
This chapter explains how you can start working toward your retirement
savings goal, regardless of your current income level. It discusses the importance of starting with small steps, the power of saving money over time, and
strategies for finding more money to save for retirement.

At the end of the last chapter, we saw that most of the providers we surveyed knew that
they should be saving more money for retirement, but most of them had few or no plans to
do so. Why not? Our survey allowed respondents to choose more than one answer to this
question—57% responded that they had too many bills to pay; 56% said they didn't make
enough money to save; and 20% said they didn't know how to save. Other typical barriers
to saving for retirement included statements like these:

> *My first priority is raising my children and saving for their college education.*

> *My family is having a financial crisis* [major medical bills, credit card debt, loss of
> spouse's job, death of spouse, etc.]*, and there's no money left over for saving.*

> *My income is too unstable to put aside any savings because the demand for child
> care in my area keeps going up and down.*

Sound familiar? Since most of these reasons are based on a lack of money, let's examine that
issue more closely.

Can You Afford to Save for Retirement?

It's true that many providers earn a low income, which makes it more difficult to accumulate substantial savings for retirement. In our survey, 74% had made a net profit of less than
$20,000 in the previous year. Only 5% had made a profit of $40,000 or more. In this situation, daily expenses can leave little money left to save, for retirement or any other purpose.
However, this doesn't mean that you need to give up on saving for retirement until your
financial situation improves.

In chapter 1, I suggested that you complete an exercise in tracking your spending and offered some strategies to help you spend less money. (If you skipped that exercise, you may want to go back and do it after reading this chapter.) In my workshops, I find that most providers who complete that exercise, regardless of their income level, end up realizing that there *are* some ways that they can reduce their expenses and put more money into savings.

The most important factor isn't whether you have the *money* to save; it's whether you have the *will* to save. You need to believe that saving for retirement is a higher priority than some of your current spending.

Saving for your long-term needs will take initiative, planning, and perseverance—so can you do it? Of course! How do I know that? Because these are exactly the same skills that it takes to run a family child care business. You took the *initiative* to start your own business, you continually *plan* your program and activities, and it requires great *patience and perseverance* to care for children and help them develop.

Take the First Steps Now

In my workshops, I've heard all kinds of excuses for why providers don't make saving for retirement a higher priority. But when it comes right down to it, most of these reasons boil down to an inner voice that says "I just can't"—when, in fact, you can.

If you don't think you have the knowledge needed to invest for retirement, you can acquire it. You can educate yourself about investing and saving. You can take your first steps now, regardless of your income level. If you don't know where the money will come from, this chapter (and Part I of this book), will give you many suggestions to try out.

If you don't understand how investments work, chapter 14 will teach you what you need to know now and explain how to learn more. If you don't know where to invest your money, chapter 15 will guide you in getting started. If you don't know what an IRA is, chapter 16 will explain the major IRA plans and help you choose the best one for your situation.

You don't need to know all the answers now; you just have to take some first steps and start educating yourself. The only strategy that definitely won't work is ignoring your future and hoping that it will somehow take care of itself.

Family child care providers are smart. You know that you should be saving more money for retirement. However, planning for retirement often means acknowledging that, if you don't change your ways, you may have to work after retirement, lower your standard of living, or both. If you have completed the retirement planning worksheet in the previous chapter, then you have already faced that reality. (Congratulations! That's often the hardest part of the process.)

Nevertheless, many people find it too difficult to take that first step, so they turn their heads away and just cross their fingers that their retirement needs will be resolved some-how, as if by magic. However, you don't have to win the lottery or even make just a little more money before you can start saving for retirement. The secret to saving more is simply believing that you *can* plan for the future, start now, and improve your situation.

People who educate themselves about their future financial needs are more likely to take steps to meet those needs. If you plan ahead and set some financial goals for yourself, you'll probably achieve your goals; even if you miss them, you'll be further ahead than you are now. If you don't set any goals, nothing is likely to change. You can't reach a goal that you haven't made.

Start with Small Steps

A big change is a lot easier to make if you start with small steps. This is especially true when you're trying to develop new habits that will help you reach a long-term goal. The quickest way to fail at saving for retirement is to set an overly ambitious initial goal and then get discouraged when you fall short. Start by regularly setting aside a small amount of money, whatever you can spare now. Once you get into the habit of saving, slowly increase your deposits.

When we asked our survey respondents to advise other providers on how to build their retirement savings, they emphasized again and again the importance of starting with small steps:

Start saving right away, even if you can only put aside $10 a month at first. At least you have started, and you can increase it as you are able.

When you first start working, regardless of what you're making, put a little bit aside for retirement every time you get paid. Get used to putting it away, and you'll never miss it—treat it just like just another bill to pay.

Make a plan, and stick with it early in life, even if it only means saving $20 a week. That's what I wish I would have done!

Save at least something every month, even if it's just a little bit—and then leave it alone and don't touch it.

To all my friends in this business—even putting away just $10 a week will add up to $520 at the end of the year. And that small money will start working for you and turn into big money that will support you when you can't work any more. Always remember that small money will make big money if you leave it untouched.

How Money Grows Over Time

How can you turn "small money" into "big money"? The secret is to start saving *now*—because when it comes to saving for retirement, time really *is* money. The reason for this is that the more time you have to save money, the faster it will accumulate each year. For example, if you invest $5,000 and it earns 8% a year, at the end of the first year you will have $5,400 ($5,000 x 108% = $5,400). If this investment also earns 8% the next year, then you will have $5,832 at the end of the second year ($5,400 x 108% = $5,832).

In this example, notice that you earned more interest in the second year than in the first year—$432 versus $400. Because of this, your effective interest rate over the 2 years was

17%, rather than the 16% you would get by just multiplying 8% by 2 years. This happened because in the second year you were earning interest on the previous year's interest. Earning interest on interest is called **compound interest**.

Although the difference made by compounding may look small in this example, as the years pass, the compound interest on your investments will grow exponentially, earning far more than you might think is possible. Let's look at an example of the power of compound interest:

- Starting at age 35, Faye saves $2,000 a year for 10 years, investing a total of $20,000. Although she stops contributing, her investments continue to grow, earning 8% per year. After 30 years, at age 65, she will have $135,042 in her retirement account.

- Starting at age 45, Faye's twin brother Fred saves $2,000 a year for 20 years, investing a total of $40,000. His investments also earn 8% per year. At age 65, he will have $91,524 in his retirement account.

Although Fred saved twice as much as Faye, he ended up with about one-third less money than she did when they both reached age 65. The reason for this shortfall is that he waited 10 more years before he started to save.

The compounding of interest over time is what causes money to grow exponentially the longer it is invested. Because of this, the best time to start investing your money for retirement is—today! And the next best time is—tomorrow! The younger you are when you start investing, the more time your investments will have to accumulate, and the more you will benefit from compounding.

Table 10. Compounded interest over time

Starting age	Annual investment	Balance at age 65
25	$1,000	$259,057
	$3,000	$777,170
	$7,000	$1,813,396
35	$1,000	$113,283
	$3,000	$339,850
	$7,000	$792,982
45	$1,000	$45,762
	$3,000	$137,286
	$7,000	$320,334
55	$1,000	$14,487
	$3,000	$43,460
	$7,000	$101,406

This table assumes that you are investing in a tax-deferred retirement fund that has an annual rate of return of 8%. It doesn't take into account the income taxes that you will need to pay when you withdraw the money from your account after retirement.

Table 10 demonstrates the power that compounding has on your investments. It shows how much you will have at age 65 depending on when you begin investing and how much you are investing annually.

Investing money early in life makes a tremendous difference. If you start investing $3,000 a year on your thirty-fifth birthday, you will have $339,850 when you reach age 65. But if you decide to put it off and wait just one year to start investing (until your thirty-sixth birthday), your balance at retirement would fall to $311,898. By putting off your $3,000 savings for one year, you have lost $27,952 for your retirement.

This example dramatically illustrates the high cost of procrastinating. But what if you're not that young anymore? Some people who are nearer to retirement don't start investing because they figure that they just don't have enough time for it to make a difference. But it's never too late in life to begin saving! If you're now age 52 and you start saving $50 a week in a tax-deferred investment that earns 8% per year, you will have $104,521 at age 70.

A Simple Rule for How Money Grows

The rule of 72 is a simple way to find out how long it will take your retirement investments to double in value. To apply this rule, divide 72 by the annual rate of return on your investment. The result will be a rough estimate of how many years it will take to double your initial investment.

For example, if you invest $1,000 in a tax-deferred investment that has an annual rate of return of 8%, the calculation would be 72 ÷ 8 = 9. This tells you that it will take about 9 years for your money to double its original value, to $2,000. Every 9 years after that, your money will double again—in 18 years, you'll have $4,000, and in 27 years, you'll have $8,000.

To motivate yourself to save your money instead of spending it, just ask yourself: Would I rather spend $1,000 today, or would I rather invest that money and give it the chance to grow to $8,000 in 27 years?

• •

Let Go of the Past

Some people find it hard to start a retirement savings plan because they keep thinking "if only": *If only I had started earlier. If only I had bought stock in 1998. If only I had listened to my spouse and not bought that boat.* But in order to plan for the future, you'll need to put the past behind you—it's done, and you can't change it. Let go of your self-judgments and forgive yourself for your past financial mistakes—then start looking forward. Look at what you've learned from your experiences, and use those lessons to make better decisions from now on.

• •

Start Saving Early!

The providers who responded to our survey repeatedly urged their peers to start saving early:

Start today! Just like children, your money needs time to grow. Before you know it, time will have flown by, and your money will be "all grown up." At some point, your body will give out, and you won't be able to work any longer. Plan for that day now.

If you only have a little bit of money to work with, don't say, "I don't have enough to amount to anything." Find a CD, and start investing a small amount. Then just watch that interest make money for you! When you notice that you didn't miss that little bit of money, you'll be ready to move on to bigger things. The younger you start, the more money you'll have for retirement—and then you'll be really happy that you did without that little bit of money when you were younger.

Try to save when you're young, because as you get older some big expense will always come up—college, a home repair, a wedding, or medical bills. Save, save, save, while you're 20 to 30 years old.

Even though it's hard to start saving for retirement, I'd suggest that you start putting a small amount away every month as soon as you're out of college.

Try to save as much as you can while you're young, and just pretend that you can't even access that money. Let the money and time work for you. Put as much as you can, as early as you can, into an IRA or a 401(k) plan.

Start early. Take charge of your own finances as a woman by managing your own bank account and your own retirement savings.

• •

Regular Saving Adds Up

If you invest just two dollars a week in a tax-deferred investment that earns 8% per year, in 20 years your savings will grow to $5,131. If you save $10 per week, your investment will grow to $25,655. At $25 a week, it will grow to $64,138.

• •

Where to Find the Money to Save

When you calculated how much money you need to save for retirement, you probably figured out that you aren't saving enough yet. By reading this chapter so far, you have (I hope) learned to start with small steps and build from there—and realized that the sooner you begin, the better. But where will the money for your first steps come from? What are some workable strategies for getting started? Here are some suggestions based on approaches that have worked for other providers.

- **Develop the savings habit**. If you're just starting to save money for retirement, the biggest challenge will be taking that first step. As we have seen, the amount you start with isn't that important—the only thing that's important is that you start saving now! The best way to establish the savings habit is to start setting aside a small amount on a regular basis, preferably weekly or monthly. Once you do that, it will be relatively easy to increase your savings whenever you can afford to do so.

    Try to save something, no matter how little. Anything is better than nothing.

    I save $1 per day per child that I care for. That goes right into my retirement account, which is currently in CDs. I also put $175 per month into an IRA, plus any extra money that I can come up with.

- **Take on a "retirement baby."** Over the years, several providers have told me that they dedicate all the income from one of the children in their care to fund their retirement account. Although setting aside the income from one child may not be enough to fully cover your retirement savings, this can be a great way to start.

    I save the money from one family for my retirement. I don't even think of spending that money because it's just for saving.

    Set aside the income from at least one child for your income and Social Security taxes. Set aside the income from another child for your retirement savings.

- **Save your Food Program income**. Another approach is to deposit your entire monthly Food Program check directly into your retirement account. Since you have already paid for the food, you might not miss it that much.

    One way I save money is by depositing my Food Program check directly into my savings account every month.

    I put my Food Program money right into my savings account, so it doesn't matter if the check is a few days (or even a week) late, since I'm not counting on it to pay my bills.

- **Make direct deposits into your retirement account**. If you normally spend all the money you earn, force yourself to start saving by setting up a recurring direct deposit that will transfer money into your retirement account on a regular basis. You can set up an automatic withdrawal plan with your investment account or your spouse's employer to withdraw a specific amount each month and transfer it into your retirement account. Providers who do this tell me that their spending drops down to the amount of cash they have in their checking account, and they don't miss what they aren't spending.

    When I worked in the corporate world, it was so much easier, because they took the savings plan money out of my paycheck every two weeks, and I didn't even notice it; now all my money goes straight to bills.

- **Dedicate any extra money to your retirement savings**. Whenever you get any "extra" money, get into the habit of putting it right into your retirement account. Do this with your tax refund, your annual rate increase, the annual Food Program rate increase, the late fees you collect from parents, and your annual registration fees.

- **Invest early in the year or regularly throughout the year**. Many people wait to put money into their retirement account until the deadline for claiming a tax deduction for their contributions (April 15 for most kinds of IRAs). However, it's a much better idea to put some money aside every month throughout the year. This is a variation on the rule "the earlier you invest, the better"—the earlier you invest *in the year*, the better.

  Here's an example. Let's say that at age 35 you decide that from now on every year you'll deposit the maximum allowable amount ($5,000) into a tax-deductible investment; for this example, we'll assume that your investment earns 8% every year.

  In the first scenario, you make your contributions on December 31 at the end of the year. In this case, 30 years later your account balance will be $566,416. In the second scenario, you contribute the same amount each year, but you spread it out and deposit $416.67 a month into your account. In this case, in 30 years you'll have $620,988. The payoff for just making your deposits on a monthly basis adds up to almost $55,000!

- **Pay yourself first**. As discussed in chapter 1, the best approach is to tuck away the savings for your own future *before* you pay your living expenses every month. This is common advice from financial planners—and other providers:

  > My financial advisor says "pay yourself first." That means putting money into your retirement account before you touch it, so you don't even miss it.

  > The best piece of advice I ever received was "pay yourself first, no matter how much or how little you're making." We contribute to a 401(k), a Roth IRA, and a SEP IRA before we pay our bills. We started with as little as $25 per month, and every year we increased it $10 or $20 a month, and now we are quite comfortable with our retirement package.

These are all very doable suggestions from other providers that can help you stash away more money in your retirement account. However, what is this retirement account that I keep talking about? Is it a regular savings account, as described in chapter 2? No, it isn't. The next step is learning where to put your retirement money. In the next two chapters I'll explain the basics of investing for the long term and show you how to choose your retirement investments. In chapter 16 I'll guide you in choosing an IRA for your investment so that you can defer paying taxes on your savings until you retire, which will allow your money to grow much faster.

Although all this may sound intimidating, if you've come this far—by estimating your retirement savings goal and choosing at least one strategy for finding money to save—you've actually done the hardest work already. Congratulations! The remaining steps will be relatively easy in comparison.

CHAPTER FOURTEEN

The Five Rules of Investing

Chapter Summary
This chapter outlines the five fundamental rules of investing. It explains how wise investors balance and diversify their investment portfolio to meet their long-term financial goals with the lowest risk and the highest return. It also explains many ways to educate yourself about investing for retirement.

Now that you know how to start saving for retirement (small), when to start saving (today), and have some ideas about where to get the money (wherever you can find it), it's time to learn the basics of long-term investing. Making smart investment decisions involves not just saving your money but also knowing where to put it. The ultimate goal is to balance the risk and return on your investments so that they will grow fast enough to meet your long-term goals with the least risk of losing the money you have invested.

Unlike some of the short-term savings options described in chapter 2, a long-term investment doesn't have a guaranteed return—there will always be some risk involved in your retirement investments. Your chances of getting a higher return on an investment will generally increase as the level of risk rises.

For example, putting your money into a savings account at your bank involves zero risk that you will lose your initial investment, since your deposit is guaranteed by the federal government. However, bank savings accounts also pay extremely low interest, so they don't allow your money to grow fast enough to satisfy your retirement needs.

If you want your money to grow into a healthy retirement fund, you'll need to learn how to choose investments that will minimize your risk and maximize your return.

The Five Rules

You work hard for the money that you earn caring for children. It's worth taking the time to learn how to invest that money so that it will work just as hard for you and be there to support you when you retire. Fortunately, making wise investment decisions isn't as complicated as you might think. There are really just five guidelines that you'll need to bear in mind:

1. Invest for the long term.
2. Balance your investments.
3. Diversify your investments.
4. Shop around to find investments with low fees.
5. Educate yourself about investing so you can understand the investments you're making.

The rest of this chapter will look at each of these rules in detail.

Rule 1: Invest for the Long Term

The first thing to learn about investing is that it is not the same thing as saving. In choosing where to put some money that you'll need in the future, you need to start by asking yourself, "When will I need this money? Is this money that I might need for a big bill or an unexpected emergency in the next few years? Or is this money that I won't need until retirement?" The answer will determine whether you want to save that money or invest it. As a rule, you want to *save* money for your short-term needs and *invest* money for your long-term needs.

- The less time before you need the money, the fewer risks you should take that it might lose value. When setting aside money for your short-term needs, your primary goal is to preserve your funds so that you can access them on short notice if needed. For this purpose, a money market fund is a good option (among others), as described in chapter 2.

- The more time before you need the money, the more risks you can afford to take with it. When setting aside money for a long-term goal—10 years or more—your primary goal is to accumulate earnings and build the value of your investment over the ups and downs of the market. To do that, you will need to put your money into one of the long-term investment options described in this chapter and the next.

Investing involves taking some risk that you'll lose money, and in return for that you expect to earn a higher rate of return over the long term. You need a higher return when investing over several years to offset the long-term effects of inflation on the value of your money.

For example, let's say that your business profit is now $20,000 a year, and you'll be retiring in 20 years. If inflation averages 4% a year, when you retire in 20 years you'll need to have an income of $43,822 just to maintain the same standard of living that you can afford today with $20,000. (In 25 years you'll need $53,317, and in 35 years you'll need $78,922.)

As we saw in chapter 11, for most people Social Security and pension benefits won't provide enough income to retire on, and you may not be able to work after retirement. So the rest of your retirement income will need to come from the growth of your investments.

If you put your retirement savings into a short-term CD or money market account, your money might (if you're really lucky) keep even with inflation, but it will have no chance of growing—you won't be able to turn "small money" into "big money," as one provider explained in the previous chapter. But when you invest for retirement, your money has to grow faster than inflation, and the only way to get that higher return is to accept some risk that the value of your investments could decline.

Don't Try to Eliminate Risk—Manage It!

Many people put off investing because they just aren't comfortable with the idea that their money might lose its value. Some people are afraid to buy stocks because they know that stocks will go up and down and may lose some or all of their value. On the news, we hear about seniors who have lost all their retirement savings because they invested in Enron, WorldCom, or some other supposedly reputable company that has gone belly-up.

You may have previously lost money in the stock market and be shy about putting any more money into stocks. Or you may not have a problem with taking a reasonable amount of investment risk but are afraid that you don't know enough and will pick the "wrong" stock to invest in.

However, when saving for retirement, you can't eliminate all risk that your investments might decline in value at some point. (Even if you stash your cash away under your mattress, there's still a risk that you could lose it to fire or theft.) More important, by avoiding investment risk, you're taking on another kind of risk that's likely to have far more serious consequences—the risk that the money you save won't grow in value and you won't end up with enough for retirement.

The best way to become comfortable with the idea of investment risk is to think in terms of managing your risk, rather than eliminating it. Instead of feeling intimidated, learn how to understand and weigh the risks you're taking when you invest your money. This will mean educating yourself about investing, as described in rule 5 below. You'll be less nervous about the possibility of losing money once you understand how you can use different kinds of investments to develop a well-rounded portfolio that has the level of risk you are comfortable with.

What's Your Risk Tolerance?

You don't have to be a poker player to save enough money for retirement. Although some investors have a higher tolerance for risk than others, the key to successful investing isn't steeling yourself to take on as much risk as possible; it's knowing the level of risk that is suitable for you. You can find this out that by taking one of the online risk tolerance surveys that are available on many of the investing sites mentioned in this book.

For example, there's a quiz on the MSN Money Web site (moneycentral.msn.com)—search the site for "Risk Tolerance Quiz." There's another good quiz located at www.icief.org/risk/risk_quiz.html. (This one is part of an online course called Investing for Success, which you may want to explore.)

Taking a risk tolerance survey will help you learn more about yourself so that you can feel more comfortable with your investment decisions. However, risk tolerance surveys don't only consider your feelings about risk; they also take into account how long you'll be investing your money.

As explained above, the level of risk you should take for a particular investment is based on your time frame for that investment. If you're in your twenties, you should be accepting a much higher level of risk for your retirement investments than your short-term savings for a down payment on a home. If you're in your forties, you should be accepting more risk for your retirement investments than for the money you're saving for your daughter's college education in 5 to 10 years. Remember: *To figure out how much risk you can afford to take, start by asking when you'll need the money*.

If you're new to investing, you may find that becoming comfortable taking risks is a long-term learning experience—it may be some time before you can invest without worrying. If you find yourself losing sleep over your investments, or if you tend to panic whenever you hear on the news that the stock market has just dropped a hundred points, then take a step back and review your plan. If your investments have a relatively high level of risk, you may want to make some changes and invest more conservatively.

However, if your investments carry a reasonable level of risk that is appropriate for your investment time frame, then you may just need more education, support, or guidance. In that case, explore the ways to educate yourself about investing described under rule 5 in this chapter. You may find that your best strategy is to ignore your feelings of panic and just leave your money alone.

Rule 2: Balance Your Investments

To minimize your risk and maximize your return, your investment portfolio will need to include the proper balance of two major kinds of investments—fixed income investments and equities.

- **Fixed income investments** are like IOUs; they are usually legal promises—typically issued by a company or a government entity—to pay you a certain amount on a certain date in the future. These investments include bonds, money market funds, and certificates of deposit (CDs). Although fixed income investments can provide a steady flow of income at a relatively low risk, their returns are also relatively low. Although their value can fluctuate over time, as a rule, the value of fixed income investments is less volatile than equities.

- **Equities** are investments in which you assume some ownership of an asset, such as a company in which you buy shares. These investments include stocks and real estate. Although the level of risk involved in different kinds of equities can vary quite a bit, overall equities offer both the highest potential returns and the highest potential risk of any kind of investment. The value of an equity asset is based on the market's assessment of its worth, and as a result, it can rise and fall quickly.

Since equities and fixed income assets offer different levels of risk and return, adjusting the ratio of these two kinds of investments in your retirement portfolio is one of the most important ways to balance the risk and return of your investments.

- You don't want to put all your money into fixed income assets because your return will be too low to beat inflation, and the earning power of your investment will gradually decline over time.

- You don't want to put all your money into equities because their value may decline abruptly just at the point when you want to start withdrawing money to live on.

As a rule, most experts advise that you maintain a balance of 60% to 70% in equities and 30% to 40% in fixed income investments, with progressively more emphasis on fixed income investments as you approach retirement. For example,

- If you're age 35 or younger, a typical balance might be 75% equities and 25% fixed income investments.

- If you're age 55 or older, your balance might be closer to 55% equities and 45% fixed income investments.

However, bear in mind that even after retirement you will still want to maintain a healthy level of investment in equities, assuming that you expect to live longer than 20 years after retiring. (And who doesn't?) If you were to convert all your investments to fixed income assets when you retire, inflation would start to erode the buying power of your savings, leaving you with a progressively lower standard of living as you grow older.

However, the above suggestions are simply a guideline—the balance of these two kinds of investments in your portfolio is ultimately up to you. In choosing your own balance, you may want to consider your risk tolerance, your age, your financial health, your physical health, your life expectancy, and how much money you want to leave to your family.

Here's a description of the three major kinds of investments in these two categories—bonds, stocks, and real estate.

Bonds

When a company or a government entity wants to borrow money, it will issue **bonds** that the public can buy. A bond is basically a promise that the issuer will pay back the amount of the bond on the bond's **maturity date**, with a fixed rate of return.

Bonds are classified by how soon they mature. You can buy **short-term bonds** (maturing in 1 to 3½ years), **intermediate-term bonds** (maturing in 7 to 10 years), and **long-term bonds** (maturing in 10 to 30 years). I discussed short-term bonds in chapter 2 as an option for short-term savings. For a long-term investment, you might choose a short-term, intermediate-term, or long-term bond, depending on your time frame and investment goal.

The amount of risk involved in a bond depends to a large degree on the length of its term. (That's why you would choose short-term bonds to minimize your risk for short-term savings.) On the other hand, long-term bonds are considered a risky investment—in fact, possibly too risky for a small investor. However, these are just some general guidelines. Since the rates of return on bonds can shift quickly, be sure to compare rates before you purchase a bond.

You can buy bonds that are issued by companies (**corporate bonds**), state and local governments (**municipal bonds**), the federal government (**treasuries**), and residential loans backed by the federal government, which are issued either by government entities or by private companies (**mortgage-backed bonds**). A bond's level of risk depends on the financial strength of its issuer.

There are many factors to consider in buying a bond. For example, you may hear that municipal bonds are the best investment because they are tax-free. However, if you follow my advice and set up all your investments as IRAs (as I'll explain in chapter 16), you'll already have a tax advantage, and it won't make any sense to buy a tax-free bond.

Stocks

When you buy a company's **stock**, you're actually purchasing a share of ownership in that company. You become a **stockholder**—and a company's management ultimately answers to its stockholders. Each year the company will describe its progress to you and other investors by issuing an annual report.

Over time, stocks are likely to earn a higher return than any other type of long-term investment, including money market funds, CDs, bonds, and real estate. However, as we know, a higher return carries with it a higher risk (Am I starting to sound like a broken record?)

A stock's value can fluctuate widely on a daily (or even an hourly) basis, based on what the public thinks the company—and therefore its stock—is worth. If the company fails to meet its financial goals, its stock will decline in value. If a company goes under, its stock can become worthless.

It may have occurred to you that if you'd only bought Microsoft stock back when the company started, you could have retired years ago. However, if you had purchased Enron stock on the same day, your retirement savings would be wiped out by now. Because of this unpredictability, buying stock in just one company is one of the riskiest kinds of investment you can make. Therefore, the stock of a particular company should never represent more than a very small part of your total portfolio. (Rule 3 will explain how to buy balanced groups of stocks to minimize your risk.)

If you're thinking of buying stock directly in one or more companies like this, bear in mind that, in addition to being risky, this is also an expensive way to invest, since you'll have to pay high broker fees and commissions.

You shouldn't invest in a company's stock until you have done thorough research to understand the company and its potential. Some new investors join an **investment club**—a group that shares the burden of researching investments and pools its members' money to buy and sell stocks. This can be a good way to learn more about investing. (For more on investment clubs, see page 138.)

Educate Yourself about Equities

As a new investor, equities may seem confusing and intimidating, and it's true that these are the riskiest and most complicated kinds of investments. However, learning about equities will pay off in the long run, since these investments also have the highest returns and will need to be an important part of your investment portfolio, even after you retire. This chapter will give you a basic introduction to investing in equities, and chapter 15 will go into more detail. After reading these two chapters, you'll have enough information to choose some basic investments so that you can get started. (You can always switch your money around later, if you wish.)

Real Estate

Buying **real estate** is another kind of equity investment, like stocks, except that in this case you will buy a share of a building or land. It's a good idea to have some money invested in real estate, since its value tends to rise when stocks fall and fall when stocks rise. (Not always, but as a general rule.) Therefore, adding real estate to your portfolio is another way to balance your risk.

Most family child care providers own their home, which is a kind of investment in real estate. However, since you'll still need a place to live after retirement, you can't consider your home to be a retirement investment unless you plan to sell it when you retire. The most common way to generate retirement income from your home is to sell it at a profit when you retire and buy a cheaper home. However, for many people this is a risky strategy, since it depends on the housing market and may not work out as you had planned.

Some people who haven't saved enough to retire on are able to get retirement income from their home in another way—they take out a **reverse mortgage**. This is a kind of mortgage that allows you to borrow money based on the value of your home. The bank pays you a set amount each month that you don't have to pay back. Then, when you die, the bank takes over ownership of your home. However, be aware that the cost of a reverse mortgage can be quite high. Before considering this option, be sure to educate yourself about its pros and cons. (The AARP Web site has some good information—www.aarp.org/money/revmort.)

Fortunately, there is a way to invest in real estate that is both more reliable and less expensive than these two options—to find out more, let's go on to rule 3.

Rule 3: Diversify Your Investments

Another important way to minimize your risk is to **diversify** your investments. What does this mean? Basically, it's a fancy word for not putting all your eggs in one basket. Here's a simple example:

Imagine that you only have two investment choices—a company that sells snow boots and a company that sells swimsuits. Which company is the better investment? The answer is that neither of them is—the best investment is to put half your money in each of these companies. Otherwise, your investment will lose value in either summer (when snow boots aren't in demand) or winter (when swimsuits aren't in demand). By putting half your money into each company, you're **diversifying** your investments—spreading your risk—to produce returns throughout the year.

This example is far more simplified than the kinds of diversification that investors look for—as you'll see in the next chapter, there are many ways to classify investments and spread your risk. Here we'll just look at the most fundamental way to diversify your fixed income investments and equities—buying into funds that have a diverse group of holdings rather than buying individual bonds, stocks, or real estate properties.

Bond Funds

As with stocks, when you buy an individual bond, you run a relatively high risk of default—if the company goes bankrupt or loses a major contract to a competitor, it may not be able to fulfill its promise to pay you back on the bond's maturity date. Purchasing bonds individually is also an expensive way to buy bonds.

A safer way to buy bonds is to invest in a **bond fund**—a professionally managed fund that invests in bonds issued by many different private and public entities. This significantly lowers your risk, because if one of the bonds goes bad, doing so will have a negligible effect on your overall investment.

There are many kinds of bond funds to choose from, but the best way to balance your risk and return is to put your money into a **bond index fund**—a fund that invests in the entire bond market. A bond index fund aims to match the performance of the broad bond market or a specific portion of that market.

The most common broad index for the U.S. bond market is the Lehman Aggregate Bond Index, which consists of corporate bonds, treasuries, mortgage-backed bonds, and some foreign bonds that are traded in the United States. Although you can't invest directly in the Lehman index, you can invest in a bond fund that will match the investments in this index. (This will be explained in more detail in the next chapter.)

Stock Mutual Funds

So you want to invest in stocks to get the higher rate of return they offer, but you also want to manage their higher risks? You may have already guessed that the best way to do this is to diversify your holdings by buying a broad range of stocks. Although you could do this by buying stock in many individual companies, that will end up being expensive, since you'll have to pay high broker fees and commissions. But, as for bonds, there's an easier and less expensive way to diversify your stock holdings—investing in a **stock mutual fund**.

Like a bond fund, a stock mutual fund is managed by professional fund managers who decide when to buy and sell different companies to maximize your profit, so you don't have to worry about researching and choosing the stocks yourself. Because of the diversification that a stock mutual fund offers, the chances of losing money in the fund are much lower than if you invest in an individual stock. Although your potential maximum return is also lower, this trade-off is usually worth it. (Unless you know what company will be the next Microsoft.)

Again, as for bonds, the best kind of stock mutual fund to buy is a **stock index fund** that aims to match the returns of a broad portion of the total stock market. We'll see why this is so important in the next chapter.

Another way to diversify your holdings and spread your risk is to invest in stock issued in other countries. Since many large U.S. companies have overseas operations, if your fund invests in U.S. companies you'll already be participating in foreign markets to some degree. However, most experts say that to be fully diversified, at least 10% of your investments should be in foreign stocks.

The next chapter will go into much more detail about stock mutual funds and stock index funds and how to choose the best investments.

• •

Does Your Spouse Own Company Stock?

Your family may own stock in an individual company if your spouse has bought stock in his employer's company through the company's retirement plan. However, bear in mind that financial experts don't recommend investing more than 10% of your retirement funds in a company where you or your spouse works. Owning stock in the same company that provides some of your income is the opposite of diversification and increases your risk, since you're putting more of your financial eggs in one basket. If the company has a bad year, your spouse could be laid off at the same time that the company's stock drops in value.

• •

Real Estate

For most people, the best way to invest in real estate for retirement is to invest in a **real estate investment trust** (**REIT**—rhymes with *neat*). This kind of investment is like a mutual fund, except that instead of buying stocks, the trust buys and manages commercial real estate, such as shopping centers, medical facilities, apartment complexes, and rental buildings. If you're a beginning investor, don't worry about investing in REITs yet; if you're a more advanced investor, see the discussion of this option in the next chapter.

Rule 4: Shop Around for Low Fees

When choosing investments, it's essential that you shop around and choose investments that have low expenses. As we'll see in the next chapter, the expenses associated with a fund are the most important indicator of how well that investment will perform, or maximize your return. As a rule, the higher the investment fee, the lower your return.

Just remember: *Whenever you have to pay higher expenses for an investment, you are reducing your return without reducing your risk.*

Any time you buy an investment—whether a stock or bond mutual fund or a REIT—make sure that you understand all the fees associated with that investment. Always look for "no-load" funds, which don't charge a commission when you buy or sell.

Although funds are required to disclose all their fees and expenses, the disclosures may be so buried in the fine print that they can be hard to find, so you do have to watch out for hidden expenses. (Also, when you review the earnings history for a potential investment, be sure to check if the numbers shown are before or after expenses.)

Although this may sound a bit scary, it actually isn't that difficult to find funds that have low fees. As a rule, index funds (for stocks or bonds) charge lower fees that enable them to outperform most other mutual funds. Therefore, investing in an index fund will give you the best chance of achieving the highest return at a relatively low risk, thus maximizing the performance of your investments. I'll explain all of this in more detail in the next chapter.

Rule 5: Educate Yourself about Investing

The more you understand about your investments and the way the market works, the more confident you'll be in your decisions, and the better decisions you will be able to make. Most of us weren't taught by our parents how to save for retirement—and this topic usually isn't covered in high school or college either. As a result, most people have very low financial literacy. The only way to change this is to take responsibility for educating yourself—about money in general, and investing for retirement in particular. Other providers agree:

> *Keep yourself open for knowledge and education. I don't know it all, and I might not be doing it right—so I need to find out how to do it right!*

> *Take a college course in personal finance, and read as much as you can about financial matters.*

> *I've had some kind of retirement account since I started doing child care, and I'm so glad that I did. Some people see their child care income as extra spending money—and that's exactly what they do with it, spend it all!*

Some people turn to a financial planner to help them understand how to meet their retirement goals. I'll discuss later how to find and work with a financial advisor. But even if you hire a professional advisor, you can't turn over all the responsibility for your investment decisions to her. You need to know enough to understand her recommendations—and the best way to do that is to learn the basics of investing and retirement planning.

Reading this book is a good place to start; here are some more suggestions for educating yourself further:

- **Know your own investments**. The first rule of investing is *Don't buy any investments that you don't understand*. Before you make any investment, do research and ask questions until you are satisfied that you understand the balance of risk and return involved in that investment. You should be completely familiar with every investment in your portfolio and know how it fits into your long-term plan. (If there's anything that you don't understand in your quarterly statement, don't hesitate to ask your investment company or financial advisor to explain it to you.)

- **Read the financial pages in your newspaper**. The Sunday edition of the *Wall Street Journal* includes a "Personal Finance" section that has very helpful articles about a range of financial situations. You can read these articles on the Web at www.sunday.wsj.com. Some local newspapers reprint these articles in their Sunday edition (and you can probably also find the *Wall Street Journal* in your local library). Even if your local newspaper doesn't carry these articles, it will probably offer other columns or articles about personal finance and investing.

- **Read a magazine**. There are several magazines on investing and money management that you can read online or at your local library. These include *Kiplinger's Personal Finance* (www.kiplinger.com), *SmartMoney* (www.smartmoney.com), and *Money Magazine* (money.cnn.com—click on Personal Finance and then on Money Magazine). I suggest that you read these magazines for their financial management advice, which can be very helpful, rather than for their investment recommendations, which aren't very reliable.

- **Read a book**. There are several excellent books on personal finance and retirement planning, including *Personal Finance for Dummies* by Eric Tyson, *Making the Most of Your Money* by Jane Bryant Quinn, and *How to Turn Your Money Life Around* by Ruth Hayden. (These books and several others that I recommend are listed in the appendix.)

• •

Don't Believe Everything You Read
Although it's a good idea to read as much as you can about investing in newspapers, magazines, and books and on the Web, bear in mind that authors and reporters aren't accountable for what they write. Also, beware of anyone who has a financial stake in what they are advising you to do. Before taking action, weigh the advice and compare it with information from other sources, or discuss your plans with a qualified financial advisor.

• •

- **Take a class**. You can take a personal finance or retirement planning class offered by a local community college or university, or you can attend a seminar offered by a local financial planner. However, if you take a workshop sponsored by a financial planner, don't buy any financial products that the speaker may be trying to sell you until you know more about investing and retirement planning. Just use the seminar as an opportunity to further your education.

- **Educate yourself about the retirement issues that women face**. Women need to be more careful about saving for retirement than men, because they typically have lower incomes than men and they live longer than men. (On average, a woman who is age 65 in 2008 can expect to live to age 85, and life expectancies are continuing to rise.) There are some retirement Web sites that focus specifically on the issues faced by women, including the Women's Institute for a Secure Retirement (www.wiserwomen.org) and the Women's Institute for Financial Education (www.wife.org/money_retirement.htm).

- **Consider joining an investment club**. An investment club is a group of people who get together to pool their money and invest in the same funds. If there's a club in your area, you may not even know it, since by law these clubs aren't allowed to recruit members. However, you can approach a club and ask to join it.

    To locate an investment club in your area, visit the Web site for the National Association of Investors Corporation (www.betterinvesting.org). You may also want to search Google Groups (groups.google.com) for discussion groups that are focused on investment clubs. For more information about joining an investment club, see www.investopedia.com/articles/01/062001.asp.

- **Contact your local extension agent**. The cooperative extension system is a nationwide, noncredit educational network that is affiliated with each state's land-grant university. There are extension offices throughout every state, and these offices can provide helpful information about a range of topics, including personal finance. You might ask your local extension agent if he can provide any educational materials on financial planning. To find an extension office near you, visit www.csrees.usda.gov.

- **Bookmark your favorite financial Web sites**. You can find excellent resources for just about any financial topic online. In addition to the links listed in the above suggestions, the retirement calculator sites listed in chapter 12 also offer extensive financial planning information. Here are some other good Web sites that you may want to check out:

    - MSN Money: moneycentral.msn.com
    - TIAA-CREF: www.tiaa-cref.org
    - Financial Engines: www.financialengines.com
    - The National Retirement Planning Coalition: www.retireonyourterms.org
    - Morningstar: www.morningstar.com
    - Retire Early: www.retireearlyhomepage.com
    - Kiplinger: www.kiplinger.com
    - America Saves: www.americasaves.org
    - Consumer Reports: www.consumerreports.org

You can also find extensive resources for educating yourself about retirement planning and investment on the Web sites of the large investment companies that I'll discuss in chapter 15. (To sort through all these online resources, you may want to consult the appendix, which lists all the Web sites mentioned in this book by chapter and topic.)

CHAPTER FIFTEEN

Choosing Your Investments

Chapter Summary
This chapter explains the options for a beginning investor and shows you how to choose among them. It will give you a basic understanding of mutual funds and explain which funds produce the best return. It briefly covers some options for more advanced investors and explains how to open an investment account.

The purpose of this chapter is to give you enough information to choose the first investment for your retirement portfolio so that you can get started now. Bear in mind that this first investment doesn't have to be a permanent decision—if you change your mind after doing more research, you can always move the money into another fund without paying a penalty.

This chapter begins with an explanation of stock mutual funds that will help you understand the language that's used to describe different kinds of funds. After that I'll go into more detail about the investments that offer you the best chance of a high return at a relatively low risk—mutual funds, including index funds and life cycle funds. I'll provide some tips and recommendations for choosing from the wide range of these funds that are available. I'll also discuss some other investment options that more experienced investors may want to consider. Finally, I'll describe the difference between investments and IRAs and explain how to open your first investment account.

Stock Mutual Funds

To understand your investments, you'll need to learn some basic terms and categories that are used to describe stock mutual funds. As we saw in the previous chapter, stock mutual funds are the best way to diversify your holdings and build your nest egg fast enough to offset the effects of inflation. For this reason, the majority of your investment portfolio should consist of stock mutual funds. However, there are over 5,000 different stock mutual funds to choose from—yikes! How can you possibly sort through all those options?

One way to approach this is to understand how stock mutual funds are classified. Remember that stock mutual funds buy stock in a wide range of companies so that you don't have to worry about researching and picking individual stocks to buy. Therefore, stock mutual funds are classified based on the kinds of companies that they buy, according to two criteria:

- The **size** of the companies that the fund buys. The size of a company is described in terms of its **cap**, short for **capitalization**, which just means how much the company is worth. (However, just to make things more confusing, in practice the word *cap* is often omitted.)

- The fund's investment **style**. A fund may focus on buying companies that are in demand and potentially offer a high rate of return (**growth stocks**), companies that are selling for less and considered to be undervalued (**value stocks**), or a combination of these two approaches (**blend**).

There are three classifications in each of these two categories (size and investment style). Table 11 defines the terms that are used for these classifications.

Table 11. Categories of mutual funds

	Small	A **small (cap) fund** invests in companies that are worth between $300 million and $2 billion.
Size	Mid	A **mid (cap) fund** invests in companies that are worth between $2 billion and $10 billion.
	Large	A **large (cap) fund** invests in companies that are worth over $10 billion.
	Value	A **value fund** invests in companies that are currently considered to be a good bargain.
Style	Growth	A **growth fund** invests in companies that are experiencing rapid growth in earnings.
	Blend	A **blend fund** invests in a combination of value and growth companies.

Some mutual funds focus exclusively on a particular combination of size and investment style. For example, a **small growth fund** will focus on smaller companies that are growing rapidly (think young companies with successful new technologies). On the other extreme, a **large value fund** will look for extremely large companies that seem to be undervalued (think well-established companies in profitable but unglamorous businesses, such as boring old utilities).

A fund's holdings in these categories are described in its **prospectus**—the official description of its investment objectives, risks, expenses, and past and current performance for stockholders and potential investors. (The prospectus for each fund is updated each year and posted on the fund company's Web site; you can also order a printed copy by phone.)

A fund's prospectus will describe the size and investment style of its investment strategy in terms of the above classifications. This information is often shown using a nine-box matrix that looks something like figure 1. The filled-in box on this matrix indicates that this example is for a large blend fund. (If a fund's investment style combines various strategies, percentages may be shown in the boxes instead.)

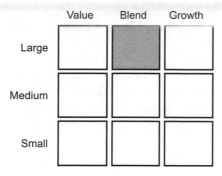

Figure 1. Investment style matrix

● ●

"Hybrid" Funds

Some mutual funds don't fit into this neat classification system. For example, a **hybrid fund** is a fund that invests in both equities and fixed income investments, such as the life cycle funds discussed later in this chapter. Here's another example:

The Pax World Balanced Fund invests 60% in equities and 40% in fixed income assets, and includes some mortgage-based bonds in its fixed income assets. (Note that a hybrid fund allows you to balance your equity and fixed income investments all in one fund.) Pax World is a socially responsible fund that has a low initial investment minimum ($250) and a low minimum after that ($50). Its management fees are also relatively low at 0.96%. For more information, visit www.paxworld. com, or call 800-767-1729.

Note: I'm including contact information for the funds discussed in this chapter to make it easier for you to learn more about potential investments. I'm not recommending that you buy or sell any of these funds.

● ●

When you choose your investments, should you try to pick the "best" of these nine categories, and then invest all your money in it? No. From year to year, different kinds of funds will perform better than others. In some years, small growth funds may outperform everything else. In other years, large value funds may be on top. Investing in mutual funds that cover a broad range of these categories will diversify your holdings and be more likely to generate higher returns than investing in fewer kinds of funds.

The best strategy is therefore to diversify your investments as much as you can across all nine categories. However, this doesn't necessarily mean that you need to have holdings in all nine categories. It just means that, as a rule, you should have money invested in mutual funds that own both large and small companies and both value and growth companies.

One way to evaluate your current holdings (or to choose investments for your portfolio) is to see how well you are diversified over these nine fund categories. For example, if you see that 80% of your investments are in large growth companies, then you're less diversified than you would be if your investments covered a broader range of companies. So to reduce your risk, you should consider rebalancing your portfolio by spreading your investments more broadly.

Index Funds

Now that you know how mutual funds are classified, let's look more closely at **index funds**, which are a specific kind of mutual fund. (So far in this chapter we have been discussing stock mutual funds; however, you can buy index funds that invest in either stocks or bonds.) As explained in the previous chapter, index funds have the lowest fees of all mutual funds, and low fees are essential if you want to maximize the return on your investments.

An index fund is a mutual fund that buys a broad range of stocks or bonds in order to match as closely as possible the returns of a specific financial market index, or **benchmark**. The fund's goal is not to try to "beat" that market but to duplicate its performance as closely as possible. The most common broad stock market indexes include the S&P 500, Russell 2000, and Wilshire 5000 indexes, each of which represents a different large category of U.S. stocks. There are also indexes for bonds and foreign stocks.

Passive and Active Investing

Why does an index fund just try to match its benchmark—why doesn't it try to outperform that benchmark? Wouldn't that be even better? Actually, no. The rationale behind index funds is based on the distinction between *active* and *passive* investing:

- Fund managers or investors who try to *outperform* the market by picking the "best" stocks are using an **active investment strategy**. Any investor who tries to make more money by regularly buying and selling her stock is using this strategy. If you're buying stock and selling it again within a year or so, then you're also an active investor.

- Fund managers who try to *match* a market index are using a **passive investment strategy**. An index fund manager buys stock that represents the fund's benchmark as closely as possible and then just holds onto it for years. For example, the manager of an S&P 500 index fund would purchase stock that represents the companies that make up that index—which happens to be the 500 largest U.S. companies—and hold onto that stock indefinitely. The fees for these funds are lower since the managers aren't actively buying and selling the stocks; they only buy and sell as needed to reflect the changing makeup of their benchmark.

Which of these two investing styles is better in the long run? You may be surprised to hear that passive investing has repeatedly been shown to be more successful.

One reason for this is that actively managed accounts have higher fees (because they are being actively managed). After taking fees into account, about two-thirds of actively managed funds don't do any better than index funds. Another reason is that the few managers who *are* able to exceed the index in any given year generally aren't able to repeat that success year after year. It's virtually impossible to pick an actively managed mutual fund that will do better than a benchmark index fund over the next year—never mind consistently over the next 20 or 30 years.

Since most actively managed funds actually do worse than the market in any given year, you'll do better in the long run by buying an index fund that will simply match the market instead.

Lower Expenses Mean Bigger Returns

As we have seen, one of the main reasons that index funds do better than other mutual funds, on average, is that they have lower annual expenses. A 2004 study by Standard & Poor's (an investment research and rating firm), found that the most important factor in the performance of a mutual fund was whether its management fees were above or below average.* This factor was more important than a fund's past performance, its fund director, or the type of companies that it invested in.

The study calculated the average expenses for nearly 17,000 mutual funds (both stock and bond mutual funds) and sorted the funds into two groups based on whether their expenses were above or below average. The average expenses charged by the higher-cost funds were 2.08% per year, while the lower-cost funds charged, on average, 0.30% to 1.06% per year.

How much does this add up to? If you invest $10,000 (a relatively small amount), your fund fees would average $200 per year for the high-fee funds and about $30 to $100 per year for the low-fee funds. The more you invest, and the longer you invest, the more these fees (and the difference between the two groups of funds) will add up.

Next, the study looked at how well the funds performed. They examined the annualized returns of all the funds over 10 years, and found that the lower-cost funds performed better than the higher-cost funds in eight of the nine investment style categories shown in figure 1. The returns of the higher-cost funds averaged 9.17% per year, while the returns of the lower-cost funds averaged 10.94% per year—for an annual difference of 1.77%.

Although 1.77% may sound like a small number, when it comes to earnings on an investment, this is a very significant difference. In our hypothetical one-year investment of $10,000, it would make a difference of $177. Multiply that by the number of years and the

---

* "Study Finds Lower-Cost Mutual Funds Prevail," The Vanguard (Autumn 2004), personal.vanguard.com/us/VanguardViews?FW_Event=vviewsnewsletters&chunk=/freshness/News_and_Views/news_ITVautumn2004_ALL_lowcost_ALL.html&Season2=Autumn&Year2=2004.

thousands of dollars that you need to save for retirement—and add the effects of compound interest—and you'll start seeing some real money.

On average, a higher-cost fund must earn 1.77% more each year than a lower-cost fund just to catch up in overall performance. Very few funds can achieve that kind of above-average return over a sustained period of time. The bottom line is that you should pay very close attention to the annual expenses charged by any fund that you are considering. You can find this information in the fund prospectus that is posted on the fund company's Web site.

How to Compare Annual Fees

Every fund prospectus includes a chart that projects how much you would have to pay in expenses on a $10,000 investment over 1, 3, 5, and 10 years. When comparing these numbers, use the 10-year number whenever possible. However, bear in mind that these numbers are projected based on the current fees, so your actual fees over the years may be different. (You can also look on the Internet for sites that will help you compare expenses from one fund to another.)

Here's an example of how to compare the fees for two funds: The Third Avenue Value Fund (a small cap value fund; www.thirdavenuefunds.com) shows a 10-year expense projection of $1,352, based on an annual operating expense of 1.06%. Let's see how well that compares to an index fund that tracks a benchmark of small cap value companies. The Vanguard Small Cap Value Index Fund (www.vanguard.com) has 10-year expenses of $293, with an annual operating expense of 0.23%.

This amounts to a difference of $1,059 for every $10,000 that you invest for a 10-year period. If you invested $100,000 for 20 years, you'd be projected to end up paying $27,040 in expenses for the Third Avenue fund versus $5,860 for the Vanguard fund.

This great disparity over time is based on the 0.83% difference in annual expenses (1.06% versus 0.23%). Because of it, the Third Avenue fund would have to earn almost 1% more than the Vanguard fund every year just to stay even with the Vanguard fund's performance.

Index funds have low annual operating fees because their overhead is lower. Since they follow a passive investing model, they don't need to pay sky-high salaries to their fund managers—investments are bought and sold only as needed to follow the index more closely. Since the investments in your index fund aren't being bought and sold on a regular basis, your expenses will reflect lower transaction fees and taxes.

Comparing Index Funds

Investing in an index fund sounds like a simple proposition—but even after narrowing your choices down to an index fund, there are still hundreds of funds to choose from. You can buy index funds that track small companies, large companies, foreign companies, utility companies, growth companies, and so on. However, to pursue the goal of balancing risk and return by investing in the broad market, I suggest that you look for an index fund that tracks a broad market benchmark.

There are five major U.S. indexes that represent a broad market in stocks or bonds. Most mutual fund companies offer index funds that track each of these benchmarks:

- The Wilshire 5000. This index tracks the entire U.S. stock market.

- The S&P (Standard and Poor) 500. This index tracks the 500 largest U.S. companies.

- The Russell 2000. This index tracks the smallest 2,000 of the 3,000 largest U.S. companies.

- MSCI EAFE (Morgan Stanley Capital International Europe, Australasia, and Far East). This index is the most commonly used benchmark for foreign stock funds.

- The Lehman Brothers Aggregate Bond Index. This index tracks a combination of U.S. government bonds (treasuries), corporate bonds, and mortgage-backed bonds.

There are many investment companies that offer index funds. To show you how to compare the funds that you are considering at different mutual fund companies, I'm going to use some of the broad-market index funds offered by four major investment companies—Fidelity, Charles Schwab, T. Rowe Price, and Vanguard.

These four companies all offer a wide range of index funds as well as actively managed funds. Because each company offers so many different choices, you can probably find one or more funds that suit your needs at any of these four companies. The comparison of these companies is shown in table 12.

As the table shows, all of these companies offer funds that track the same—or a very similar—benchmark. However, just because two funds are both tracking the same index doesn't mean that your investment returns will be identical. For one thing, the fund's management fees may be different. For another, they may be using slightly different strategies to reach the benchmark.

As you can see, although the fees for index funds are quite low on average, they do vary—so be sure to compare fees, even when shopping for an index fund. Although Fidelity has the lowest management fees for three out of the five funds, it also has the highest minimum investments. Charles Schwab has the lowest minimum investments, but the highest management fees. Vanguard has the lowest fees if you look at the average across all five funds.

Since the goal of these funds is to match the market, if you invest in any of these index funds your investments won't outperform the market average, but they will most likely beat a large majority of actively managed mutual funds. As we have seen, trying to pick a winning individual mutual fund isn't likely to succeed. Low-cost, passive investing is the safest way to get a reasonable return at a low risk.

Table 12. Comparing selected index funds

Benchmarks	*Fidelity*	*Charles Schwab*	*T. Rowe Price*	*Vanguard*
Wilshire 5000 (or similar index)	Spartan Total Market Index Fund Fee: 0.10%	Schwab Total Stock Market Index Fee: 0.53%	Total Equity Market Index (Wilshire 4,500 Completion Index) Fee: 0.40%	Vanguard Total Stock Market Index Fund Fee: 0.19%
S&P 500	Spartan 500 Index Fund Fee: 0.10%	Schwab S&P 500 Index Fund Fee: 0.36%	Equity 500 Index Fee: 0.37%	Vanguard S&P 500 Investor Shares Fee: 0.18%
Russell 2000	Fidelity Small Cap Retirement Fund Fee: 1.04%	Schwab Small-Cap Index Fund Fee: 0.57%	Small-Cap Stock Fee: 0.91%	Vanguard Small-Cap Index Fund Fee: 0.23%
MSCI EAFE (or similar index)	Spartan International Index Fund Fee: 0.10%	Schwab International Index Fund (Schwab International Index of the 350 largest foreign companies) Fee: 0.69%	International Equity Index Fund (FTSE Developed ex North America Index) Fee: 0.52%	Vanguard Total International Stock Index Fund (MSCI Europe Index, MSCI Pacific Index & MSCI Emerging Markets Index) Fee: 0.32%
Lehman Bond Index	Fidelity U.S. Bond Market Index Fee: 0.31%	Schwab Total Bond Market Fund Fee: 0.53%	US Bond Index Fee: 0.30%	Vanguard Total Bond Market Index Fee: 0.20%

Investment information

	Fidelity	*Charles Schwab*	*T. Rowe Price*	*Vanguard*
Minimum initial investment for IRA	$10,000 ($500 for a SEP IRA)	$100	$1,000	$3,000
Minimum additional investment	$1,000	$1	$50	$100
Contact information	www.fidelity.com 800-343-3548	www.schwab.com 866-232-9890	www.troweprice.com 800-922-9945	www.vanguard.com 877-662-7447

Note: The above information is accurate as of July 2008; check current information and fees before investing.

Life Cycle Funds

Rule 2 in the last chapter explained the importance of balancing your investments in equity and fixed income assets. Let's say that when you initially choose your investments, you take this into account by investing 70% of your funds in a stock fund and 30% in a bond fund. However, as the years go by, this ratio will change as the stock and bond markets rise and fall. After five years, you may discover that you are actually invested 78% in stocks and 22% in bonds.

To maintain your target ratio of 70% stocks and 30% bonds, you'd need to rebalance your portfolio by selling some of your investment in the stock fund and increasing your investment in the bond fund. If you don't do this, your portfolio will continue to shift away from your original balance, and your investments will no longer have the balance of risk and return that you're aiming for. In addition, as you grow older, your target ratio will change, since it's desirable to incur less risk as you approach retirement and prepare to withdraw some of your funds.

In the past, investors have had to review their holdings every year and move their money around to maintain the balance they were aiming for. However, recently a new kind of fund has become popular that takes care of this rebalancing for you. A growing number of employer-sponsored 401(k) and 403(b) plans are offering these "life cycle" or "targeted" funds as an option. These funds have become quite popular with people who don't want to have to worry about rebalancing their investments.

To select a **life cycle fund**, you start by identifying the **target date** that you expect to retire, say 2030. You then pick a life cycle fund that aims for that retirement date. The fund's managers will continually rebalance the fund for you, maintaining the optimal ratio of stocks and bonds as you approach retirement. The fund will originally have a higher percentage of stocks than bonds, but will gradually move toward bonds as the target retirement year approaches.

Disadvantages of Life Cycle Funds

Although life cycle funds are popular, they do have some disadvantages. For one thing, managing your holdings purely on the basis of your age is a problematic approach, since it doesn't take into account any individual considerations, such as your assets and debts, marital status, health, financial goals, risk tolerance, or when you will need the money. Other potential issues exist:

- You may not be able to find a life cycle fund that matches the exact year that you wish to retire.

- Some life cycle funds don't invest in low-cost index funds; therefore their fees are higher.

- The investments in your life cycle fund may overlap with your other investments, making your portfolio less diversified (and therefore more risky).

- The fees for life cycle funds are likely to be higher than those for index funds.

Before investing in a life cycle fund, examine its fees and evaluate how much risk the fund is taking—the higher the percentage of fixed income funds, the lower the risk.

Table 13. Comparing selected life cycle funds

	Fidelity Freedom 2030	Schwab Aim Independence 2030	T. Rowe Price Retirement 2030	Vanguard Target Retirement 2030
Investment style	Large cap growth	Doesn't fit any specific style	Large cap growth	Large blend
Asset allocation	82% stock 18% fixed income	73% stock 27% fixed income	91% stock 9% fixed income	90% stock 10% fixed income
Initial minimum investment	$200	$100	$1,000	$3,000
Subsequent minimum investment	$100	$1	$50	$100
Management fee	0.80%	0.96%	0.76%	0.21%
Management fees on $10,000 over 10 years	$990	$1,264	$942	$268

Note: The above information is accurate as of July 2008; check current information and fees before investing.

Comparing Life Cycle Funds

When choosing a life cycle fund, bear in mind that two life cycle funds aren't interchangeable just because they are targeting the same retirement year. Even though their target retirement date is the same, the companies that offer the funds may have different investment strategies and goals. The two funds are also likely to have different fees and required minimum investments.

To clearly see the differences between the life cycle funds you're considering, I suggest that you create a comparison chart like the one shown in table 13. This chart compares the life cycle funds for the target year 2030 issued by the four major investment companies that we compared in table 12 on page 148. Bear in mind that the table shows how each of these funds is allocating their investments as of 2007—all of these funds will shift toward fixed income investments as the year 2030 approaches.

If you were trying to choose between these four life cycle funds, you would want to note and weigh the following differences:

- The Schwab and Fidelity funds have lower initial minimum investments.

- The Schwab fund has the most conservative investment allocation and the highest fees.

- The Vanguard fund has the highest initial investment minimum, but it's more diversified (investing in small cap stocks as well as large companies), and it has the lowest fees.

In reading the fund descriptions, you would also notice that the Vanguard fund invests mostly in U.S. and international index funds, while the other funds are putting only a small fraction of their investments into index funds.

Since these four funds are following different investment strategies, they will have different returns in the year 2030. Although we can't predict their performance between now and 2030, we can compare their expenses. Remember investment rule 4—whenever you have to pay more for an investment, you're reducing your return without reducing your risk. So how do these four funds stack up?

When we calculate the charges on a $10,000 investment over 10 years, the Vanguard fund charges the least, about $1,000 less than Schwab and $700 less than the other two. (Fidelity, Schwab, and T. Rowe Price generally have higher fees for their life cycle funds than their other index funds, while Vanguard's fees remain about the same. That's because the Vanguard life cycle funds invests more in index funds than the other life cycle funds.)

Over time, the differences in these fees can add up to quite a lot. If you invested $50,000 in the Vanguard fund for 20 years, you could expect to save about $7,000 in fees compared with the Fidelity or T. Rowe Price funds—and about $10,000 compared with the Schwab fund. That's a big difference! Of course, in the year 2030 the return on these four funds could vary greatly, and in theory that could make up for the big difference in fees, but we don't have any way to predict that.

Employer 401(k) and 403(b) Plans

I mentioned in chapter 11 that employers are increasingly offering employee 401(k) and 403(b) plans instead of pensions. These retirement plans are actually investment plans that offer the same tax benefits as an IRA (as explained in the next chapter).

If you or your spouse is eligible to participate in an employer-sponsored retirement plan, you should take full advantage of its benefits. Some employers will automatically contribute part of an employee's salary to the plan as a substitute for a traditional pension. Others will match an employee's contributions up to a certain percentage.

Be sure to contribute enough to receive any maximum matching funds that your employer offers—even if the investment choices aren't the best, this is "free money" toward your retirement that you shouldn't pass up. (First get the match, and then see if you can move the money to a better investment later.)

Learn the options offered by the employer's plan. For example, a growing number of employer retirement plans are offering index funds as one of the investment choices. Some plans will allow you to "roll over" your plan money into another IRA even while you're still participating; others won't. If you or your spouse leaves the company, you'll have the option of rolling over your funds to another IRA, and you may also have the option of keeping your money in the plan.

If you have the choice, should you leave your money in the employer's plan, or should you do a rollover? Unfortunately, there's no easy answer to this question. If your investments are doing well, then you may not want to move them. However, you may want to consider rolling over your money into another IRA under these circumstances:

- Your choices in the employer's plan are limited. (For example, there are no index funds to choose from.)

- The mutual funds you can choose from are not performing well compared to their benchmarks.

- The management fees for the funds in the employer's plan are a lot higher than the fees for index funds.

If you're allowed to do a rollover, you can move your money into any other investment, such as any of the index funds described above. First, pick the fund you wish to invest in and what kind of IRA you want it to be (see below), then ask the employer for the paperwork you'll need to transfer your money into the new fund.

If the employer matches your retirement contributions and you transfer your money to another plan while you or your spouse is still working there, be sure to keep contributing enough to the employer's plan to continue receiving the maximum matching funds.

More Advanced Investment Options

Since so many family child care providers are new to investing, our discussion so far has been pretty basic. If you're a more advanced investor, none of this will be new to you. In that case, here are a few options that you may want to consider, if you haven't done so already. If you're a beginning investor, don't worry about these options—until you know more, just stick with the basic choices outlined above.

Real Estate Investment Trusts (REITs)

In rule 2 in the last chapter, I explained that to diversify your holdings and spread your risk, it's helpful to have some of your equity investments in real estate as well as stocks. This lowers your overall risk, since these two investments tend to move in opposite directions. In rule 3, I mentioned that the best way to invest in real estate is to buy a **real estate investment trust** (REIT).

A REIT uses the money from its investors to buy and manage commercial real estate property. Buying real estate through a REIT is less risky and less work than owning and managing a rental property yourself. There are REITs that specialize in apartment houses, office buildings, hotels, and other commercial properties. However, to reduce your risk, it's best to invest in a REIT that owns a diversified portfolio of all kinds of real estate properties.

To minimize the fees for your REIT, look for investments that use the indexing approach, as for stocks. Here are some examples of REIT index funds:

- Vanguard REIT Investor Shares: This fund tracks the MSCI US REIT Index. There is a $3,000 minimum initial investment for IRAs and a $100 minimum investment after that. The expense ratio is 0.21%, with an additional $20 annual fee for a Roth or regular IRA ($25 for a SIMPLE IRA) if you invest less than $10,000 (www.vanguard.com).

- Wells S&P REIT Index Fund (Class A no load): This fund tracks the S&P REIT Composite Index. The expenses are a 4% sales charge when you buy the fund and a 0.99% annual expense ratio (www.wellsref.com).

- DJ Wilshire REIT EFT: This fund tracks the Dow Jones Wilshire REIT Index and has a 0.25% expense ratio (www.amex.com).

Note: Although Fidelity and T. Rowe Price also offer real estate funds, they don't offer any real estate index funds.

Exchange Traded Funds (ETFs)

An **exchange traded fund** (ETF) operates like an index fund by tracking the performance of a specific benchmark. The difference is that an ETF is itself traded like a stock on the stock exchange. This provides the diversity of an index fund with the added feature of being able to buy and sell throughout the day. You can buy ETFs that track different benchmarks, such as international stocks, REITs, or bonds. One of the most popular ETFs is the SPDR ("Spider"), which tracks the S&P 500 index.

Although ETFs have much lower fees than most mutual funds, you will pay a brokerage fee each time you buy or sell. The more you trade, the higher your fees. If you are investing more often than on a monthly basis, these brokerage fees can cause your total fees to exceed those of most regular index funds and even most mutual funds.

An ETF is probably worth considering only if you have a lump sum you want to invest and you do not plan to add to it regularly. If you do plan on adding to your investment account on a regular basis, compare all the fees involved before choosing to invest in an ETF. As the ETF brokerage fees rise, you may decide it makes more sense to stick with a regular index fund.

Annuities

For many seniors, the biggest fear is that their income stream will run out at some point after they retire. Even if your investments are well-diversified, a big jump in inflation or a large drop in the stock market could have a negative effect on all of your investments at the same time and lower your income. If this happens during your first years in retirement, it could severely disrupt your life. For example, your investment returns will be diminished if you have to sell stocks while the market is down. But what if you could buy insurance that would guarantee that the money you have saved for retirement will generate income as long as you live? To get this kind of peace of mind, more people are turning to **annuities**.

Annuities are insurance products sold by investment companies that can give you a guaranteed stream of income for life. When you purchase an annuity, you're buying insurance to cover the risk that your money won't last long enough. It's one of the few financial tools that can provide you and your spouse with income for as long as you live. There are two types of annuities—immediate and deferred.

With an **immediate annuity**, you turn over a certain amount of your retirement savings, and within a year the company starts sending you a monthly check for as long as you live. The amount you receive each month is guaranteed, regardless of the inflation rate or what happens to the stock market. The amount of your monthly check is determined at the time you buy the annuity and will depend on how much you initially invest, your age, your life expectancy, and the current interest rates. Most people don't buy an immediate annuity until they are ready to retire.

A **deferred annuity** is a tax-deferred savings plan that will start paying you at a specific date in the future. Since the taxes are deferred, you won't have to pay any taxes on the money you save until you withdraw it. When the annuity payments start, you can decide whether to receive a guaranteed fixed amount or a variable amount (a variable annuity). If you buy a **variable annuity**, the amount of your payments will depend on how well your investments in the annuity are performing, so you'll be assuming some risk that your payments could be reduced.

Beyond these basics, annuities can get very complicated. There are many kinds of annuities you can get to meet your individual needs. You can buy an option that will guarantee a payout to your spouse if you die. You can buy a variable annuity that guarantees you a minimum payment regardless of how well your investments are performing. Another option will allow you to access your money sooner if you're diagnosed with a serious illness that's likely to shorten your life. There are even indexed annuities that offer payouts linked to the performance of a stock index, such as the S&P 500, but that also offer a guaranteed minimum return. The list of annuity options is extensive.

As a rule, it isn't a good idea to invest all your retirement savings in an annuity. It does make sense to put part of your money into an annuity as you approach retirement, in order to get more security and a steady stream of income. However, even at that point, you don't want to put all your money into annuities because the value of the annuity payments is likely to be eroded by inflation. You'll still need a balanced portfolio in order to take advantage of the higher return offered by equities.

Most major investment and insurance companies offer annuities. When shopping for an annuity, consider the amount of the payout, the long-term financial strength of the company that is offering the annuity, and the fees and commissions that are being charged.

Since there are so many different options for annuities, make sure that the options you're considering meet your individual needs. Here are some online resources that can help you learn more about annuities:

- Annuity FYI: www.annuityfyi.com

- Insurance Information Institute: www.iii.org/Individuals/annuities

- Association for Insured Retirement Solutions: www.navanet.org

- U.S. Securities and Exchange Commission (on variable annuities): www.sec.gov/investor/pubs/varannty.htm

Since annuities are so complex, I recommend that you get professional advice about whether a particular annuity is right for you before you buy it. Look for an advisor who can clearly explain the various options and the risks associated with them. Also make sure that your advisor is primarily interested in helping you meet your needs, not in selling you a product. Before you buy any annuity, be sure you understand the risks involved in it. (Chapter 17 will explain how to find and work with a financial advisor.)

• •

The Bottom Line

Although investing for retirement is a complicated subject, I have tried to keep this discussion as simple as possible while still providing enough information to prepare you to get started making your own investment choices. Here's the bottom line:

> *The best way to minimize your risk and maximize your return is to diversify your holdings over a range of investments—fixed income assets, stocks, and real estate. Within each of these categories, diversify further by buying a low-fee index fund that follows a broad market benchmark.*

Since each person's financial circumstances are unique, there's no "one size fits all" answer to investing for retirement. The more you know, the better decisions you'll be able to make. So it's important to continue to educate yourself about investing, using the approaches listed under rule 5 in the previous chapter.

• •

Choose Your First Investments

After reading this far, you know far more about investing than most family child care providers, and you're familiar with lots of ways to educate yourself further (see rule 5). You also know enough about the basics of investing to select a basic retirement portfolio. You might choose one or more of the funds mentioned in this chapter or select from the thousands of other funds.

If you want to pick your own funds, just bear in mind the five rules discussed in chapter 14 and the major points discussed in this chapter—look for index funds with low fees. Before you buy, research the funds you are considering, and learn as much as you can about them. Remember, the key is to get yourself started. You don't have to be too obsessive about your first choice. You can always move your money to another fund later. There's usually no penalty or extra cost for moving your money to another fund, whether you're moving your money within the same family or from one company to another. (As long as you're moving the money from one IRA to another, you won't have to pay any capital gains taxes.)

Even though it's relatively easy to move your money around, it's still best to keep most of your funds at the same company, if possible. This will make it simpler to transfer your money between funds or add more funds to your portfolio.

To make sure you have enough choices, I recommend that you start with a fund (or funds) from a company that offers a wide range of mutual funds. The large companies that offer the widest range of funds include the four companies that I have used as examples in this chapter—Fidelity, Charles Schwab, T. Rowe Price, and Vanguard.

Two Options to Get Started

At this point you may feel ready to pick your own investments. Or you may still feel a bit hesitant, even though you recognize the importance of beginning to invest as soon as possible. So to make your first choice as easy as possible, I'm going to show you two suggestions that can help you get started.

Both of these suggestions include only very low-cost index funds. All of the funds are from the same company, Vanguard. Of course, that's not because I think this is the only company you should consider. I'm just doing this as an example of how you might assemble a portfolio from the funds offered by a single company.

Option 1: This is a very simple, basic option. If you just don't know where to start, you could allocate the money you have to invest in the following funds:

- 60% in the Vanguard Total Stock Market Index Investor Shares Fund
- 40% in the Vanguard Total Bond Market Index Investor Shares Fund

Option 2: This is a somewhat more diversified beginning option. You could allocate the money you have to invest in the following funds:

- 45% in the Vanguard Total Stock Market Index Investor Shares Fund
- 25% in the Vanguard Total Bond Market Index Investor Shares Fund
- 10% in the Vanguard REIT Index Investor Shares Fund
- 20% in the Vanguard Total International Stock Index Fund

Note that the balance of equity and fixed income investments shown above is a reasonable ratio for middle-aged investors who want to invest rather cautiously. If you're younger than 40, you may want to increase the percentage of your investments in stocks and real estate. If you're over 60, you may want to increase the percentage of your investments in bonds.

If you still don't feel confident enough yet to choose your investments yourself, get some help so that you can get started building your retirement nest egg as soon as possible. To do that, you could talk with a financial planner or visit a discount or full-service broker.

The Difference between Investments and IRAs

Although I've mentioned IRAs a few times, I haven't really explained them yet—that topic will be covered fully in the next chapter. At this point, you just need to know the difference between an investment and an IRA. There seems to be a lot of confusion about this—in my workshops, I'm often asked, "How much interest will my IRA earn?" or "Which IRA will earn more interest for me?" These kinds of questions reflect a common misunderstanding about IRAs and investments.

One reason for the confusion is that these two terms are often used interchangeably. For example, you may have seen advertising messages such as "Get higher interest! Make your IRA work harder!" and concluded that an IRA must be some kind of investment. However, an IRA isn't the same thing as an investment, and it won't earn you any interest.

Congress has set up **individual retirement accounts**, or IRAs, to allow you to claim tax advantages for your retirement investments—such as deducting your contributions and deferring the taxes on your earnings until you retire. These tax benefits will allow your investments to grow much faster while reducing the taxes you will owe on that money. You don't invest your money in an IRA; you invest it (typically) in stocks, bonds, or real estate. Over time, your investments will earn money, and at some point you'll need to pay taxes on those earnings.

An IRA is basically just a designation that you can use to qualify your retirement investments for these very important tax advantages. When you open an investment in a given fund, you'll identify that account as an IRA in order to get these benefits. For example, you might decide to invest in the ABC Growth Fund, the DEF Bond Fund, and the XYZ International Fund. When you open these accounts, you will designate each of them as a certain kind of IRA plan.

The different kinds of IRAs have different rules and tax benefits, as I'll explain in the next chapter. However, the kind of IRA you choose won't affect the performance of the fund you are investing in. It's your investments that will earn interest over time, not your IRAs.

So the questions you should really be asking are: "How much will my *investment* earn for me?" "Which *investment* will earn more interest for me?"

How to Get Started

Okay, let's say you've scraped together your savings and come up with $1,000 to invest. You've researched some index funds on the Web and identified the ones that you want to buy—you're ready to get started! Now what do you do?

Let's say you've chosen the ABC Fund and the DEF Bond Fund offered by the XYZ Investment Company. You could just visit the company's Web site and set up your first investments there. However, since you're a bit nervous about investing for the first time, instead of signing up online, you look up the company's phone number on the Web site and call them up.

Surprise! You get a friendly customer service representative on the phone who is more than happy to help you get started and take your money. You tell the representative that you want your $1,000 to be split between the ABC Fund and the DEF Bond Fund. The representative asks you whether these accounts should be set up as IRAs. You answer yes, you want the first fund set up as a Roth IRA and the second fund set up as a SIMPLE IRA (or whichever IRA plans you choose—the next chapter will help you decide between the various IRA plans). You then make arrangements to transfer the money into your new accounts—usually by mailing the company a check or arranging a bank or fund transfer.

That's all—you're well on your way to a more secure retirement!

You Don't Need a Lot of Money

Remember about starting with small steps? Well, maybe $1,000 doesn't sound like such a small step to you. But don't let that discourage you—there are many mutual funds that will allow you to start investing with very little money:

- TIAA-CREF will waive its regular minimum investment fee if you agree to invest at least $50 a month in an IRA account (www.tiaa-cref.org).

- Charles Schwab allows you to start investing with as little as $100 (www.schwab.com).

- Pax World will let you start with as little as $250 (www.paxworld.com).

- Morningstar has a fund screener that you can use to search for mutual funds that require an initial investment of less than $500. (Go to www.morningstar.com, click on the Funds tab, and then scroll down to find the Fund Screener in the left navigation menu.)

Remember that it's never too late to start investing for your retirement. If you start investing $25 a month now and your money earns 8% per year, after 10 years you'll have $4,574. If you invest $50 a month, you'll have $9,147—and if you invest $100 a month, it will add up to $18,295.

How Much Will Your Investments Earn?

The answer to this question is that no one really knows. In the examples of how investments grow in this book, I've used 8% to project the annual return. However, that's just a ballpark number that I've chosen to illustrate how investing works and to allow us to compare various scenarios. I'm not trying to imply that 8% is the target return that you should—or will—achieve on your investments.

I picked 8% as the ballpark number because over the entire history of the U.S. stock market, from 1802 to 1997, the average annual return was 8.4%. However, when you break this time period down into shorter spans, the average annual return varies quite a bit—for example, from 1982 through 1997, the average return per year was 16.7%. On the other hand, in 2000 the stock market went down by 6.2%, followed by a drop of 7.2% in 2001, and another drop of 16.8% in 2003.

No one knows what future returns will be. As I write this book in 2008, some financial experts are predicting that the returns over the coming decade are likely to be less than the long-term average. As a rule, I'd say that it would be too optimistic to assume that your investments will yield more than 8%. However, in estimating your potential returns, you should also consider how long you'll be investing your money. In general, the longer it will be until you need the money, the higher the estimate you could reasonably use to project your earnings.

To maximize your returns, follow the suggestions for balancing and diversifying your portfolio described above. However, bear in mind that even if you do that faithfully, your average annual return may be lower than 8%, especially if you're investing for a shorter period, such as 10 or 20 years.

Review Your Investments Once a Year

After making your initial investment, set up a plan to add to your account on a regular basis. There are various ways to do this:

- You can arrange with your investment fund to have a specific amount automatically withdrawn from your checking account on a monthly basis.

- You can make it a personal commitment to send a check to your account every month. To help you stick to your plan, you may want to schedule these deposits on the same day each month.

- If you can't commit to making a regular monthly deposit, just make a regular deposit every three or four months. The goal is to deposit money into your retirement fund on a consistent basis, year in and year out.

Also, every year—maybe at the end of the year, or on your birthday—review your progress toward your long-term goals and see how you're doing. In this review, make any adjustments needed to maintain your target balance of fixed income and equity assets.

As you approach your retirement age, you will want to increase the percentage of your investments in fixed income assets. However, always continue to keep some money invested in stock funds, since in the long run stocks will outperform all other types of investments and outpace inflation. (If you don't want to have to review your investments like this every year, then consider investing in a low-cost life cycle fund that will be continually balanced for you.)

Bear in mind that if the market goes through a bad cycle, your investments will too. Don't let that discourage you or tempt you to move your money around—remember that passive investing (buying and holding through the market's ups and downs) will yield the best results in the long run.

Since you're investing for the long term, there's also no reason to panic if the stock market goes down a hundred points or more in a day. In fact, when the stock market drops, it's actually a great opportunity for you—you'll get more value for your next regular contribution, since the price of stocks will be lower. If anything, you'll want to increase your contributions the next time the market goes down.

If you're following a passive investment strategy, as I advise, then you should also ignore all the "expert advice" about what to buy or sell that you may hear on television or read in magazines or on the Internet. Don't pay any attention to all the commentators who are urging you to get in or out of a particular stock or mutual fund based on the market's performance. As soon as you hear, "Now is the time to buy . . ." just stop listening! You don't care whether the stock market is going up or down. Regardless of how the stock market is performing, investing in low-cost, broad market index funds will serve you well. Slow, steady investing will win the day over the long term.

CHAPTER SIXTEEN

Choosing Your IRA Plans

Chapter Summary
This chapter discusses individual retirement accounts (IRAs). It outlines the
rules and benefits of the six major IRA plans and explains the importance
of the Saver's Credit for low-income families. It provides guidelines to help
you choose between the various IRA plans and prioritize your investments.

An IRA is a personal savings plan established by Congress that allows you to claim some
important tax advantages that will help your retirement investments grow faster. When you
open an investment account, you will also need to choose an IRA plan for that account.
Depending on the kind of IRA you select, you may be able to deduct some or all of your
contributions to that account on your tax return.

The primary advantage offered by most IRA plans is that they allow you to put off paying
taxes on your contributions or earnings on your investments until you withdraw the money
after you retire. This tax benefit will accumulate over time, significantly increasing the
amount of after-tax money that you'll have when you retire.

As I explained in the last chapter, I find that many people are confused about the difference between investments and IRAs. If you aren't sure that you understand the difference
between these two terms, I suggest that you review that explanation before continuing—
otherwise the discussion in this chapter may be somewhat confusing.

How IRAs Work
As we'll see below, there are many kinds of IRA plans, and each one has different rules.
However, to give you a general idea of how an IRA works, let's look at one example—a
"regular" or "traditional deductible" IRA. Although the general picture will look similar for
the other kinds of IRAs, below I'm just describing the specific rules for a traditional IRA.
We can break an IRA plan into three stages—**contributions**, **earnings**, and **withdrawals**
(also called **distributions**).

1. **Contributions**: You'll start by choosing an investment—typically a mutual fund that invests in stocks, bonds, or real estate (see chapter 15). For this example, let's say that when you open the account, you set it up as a traditional IRA. Each year after that, you can make contributions to the account, up to a certain limit. On your yearly tax returns, you will be able to deduct your contributions that year, thus reducing your federal and state income taxes.

    The amount of your tax savings will depend on your contributions and your tax bracket. For example, if you contributed $2,000 to your IRA and were in the 25% tax bracket, you'd get a tax savings of $500 that year: $2,000 x 0.25 = $500.

2. **Earnings**: Since you're investing for the long term, you'll leave your money in the investment account for years. If all goes well, your money will grow significantly over the years. As your money grows, you won't have to pay any taxes on your IRA earnings as long as your money remains invested in this account.

3. **Withdrawals**: After you retire, you'll start withdrawing funds from your investment account to pay your living expenses. Each time you make a withdrawal, the investment company will send you a form that shows the amount of the contributions and earnings included in that withdrawal. When you file your tax return that year, you'll report the total contributions and earnings you withdrew that year as income, and pay federal and state income taxes on that total.

    There are certain age limitations for withdrawing your money. As a rule, you'll have to pay a tax penalty if you withdraw money from this kind of IRA before you reach age 59½, although there are some exceptions (as explained below). You'll also have to pay a tax penalty if you don't start withdrawing certain minimum amounts at age 70½.

Why IRAs Are So Important

The above example explains generally how an IRA plan works. But is it really worth it to set up an IRA and follow all those IRS rules? Yes! Over the long term, IRAs provide you with a tremendous tax advantage for building a nest egg for retirement. To see just how large this tax advantage can be, let's compare two scenarios:

- You invest $5,000 a year and leave it in place for 20 years, but don't make your investment an IRA. Your investment earns 8% per year, but since it isn't in an IRA, you have to pay taxes on your earnings each year. If your federal and state taxes amount to 28%, after 20 years you would end up with $129,062 after taxes.

- You put $5,000 a year into the same investment, earning the same annual return (8%), but you set it up as an IRA. After 20 years, you'd end up with $228,810. If you decided to withdraw all the money at that time, paying the same 28% tax on your withdrawal, you'd still have $164,743 left over. In addition, every year the IRA was open you would have deducted your contributions, thereby reducing your income taxes. You could deposit these tax savings into another IRA or use them for any other purpose.

Although the tax deduction is one of the most important financial advantages of an IRA, for this comparison we'll just look at the after-tax amounts you'll have left after 20 years. In the second scenario, you have earned about 28% more after taxes simply by calling your investment an IRA, not counting the tax savings from your yearly deductions. In the context of investing for retirement, that's a big, big difference.

Allowing your contributions to grow tax-deferred over many years will generate significant savings for you. Therefore, in order to maximize your retirement savings, you should take full advantage of the IRA options available to you and put as much of your retirement investments as possible into IRAs. (Or into an employer's 401(k) or 403(b) plan, if you or your spouse is employed—these plans offer the same tax benefits as an IRA.)

Although there are maximum limits on the amount you can contribute to certain IRAs each year, there's no limit on how many different IRA accounts you can have. You're likely to end up with more than one IRA account if:

- Your spouse has moved from job to job, and you're holding onto different IRAs from his previous employers.

- You want to diversify your investments, so you have (for example) one IRA account for a stock fund and another one for a bond fund.

However, since diversification is an important principle of investing for retirement, you could well end up with not just 2, but 3, 4, 5, or even more IRA accounts in your portfolio. In fact, the only time you would have just one IRA for all your retirement savings would be if you were putting all your investments into a life cycle fund, as described in the previous chapter.

• •

You Can't Make an Existing Investment an IRA

You have to identify an investment as an IRA when you set it up; you can't turn an investment that you already have into an IRA. If you wanted to make an existing investment an IRA, you'd first have to withdraw the money you want to transfer. Then you'd have to reinvest that money into another account that you have set up as an IRA. (You could put the money back into the same fund, but it would have to be in a new account.)

It's always a good idea to transfer any money you're saving for retirement out of a taxable account into an IRA, since your earnings will then be tax-deferred, allowing your money to grow much faster over time. Even if you end up having to pay some taxes because you transferred the funds, the long-term tax savings from putting the money into an IRA will be well worth it.

• •

The Six Major IRA Plans

This section describes the six IRA plans that you can choose from if your business is set up as a sole proprietorship—a business operated by a self-employed person—as most family child care businesses are. (Otherwise, see the box below.) I'll start with an outline of the six options, and then discuss how they compare to each other. The six options are these:

- traditional deductible (regular) IRA
- traditional nondeductible IRA
- Roth IRA
- SIMPLE IRA
- SEP IRA
- self-employed 401(k) plan

As you read the description of each plan, bear in mind that I'm describing the rules that were in effect as of July 1, 2008; some of the rules and limits described here could change by the time you read this book.

• •

If You Aren't Self-Employed

Although most family child care providers operate their business as a sole proprietor (self-employed person), some providers form a partnership with another provider or structure their business as a corporation to reduce their taxes and personal liability.

- If you are a partner in your business, you have all the IRA options identified below, with the exception of the self-employed 401(k) plan.

- If your business is incorporated, you have the same IRA options as a self-employed person. Your corporation could also establish a corporate 401(k) plan.

As a rule, I recommend that family child care providers operate as a sole proprietorship. Forming a partnership or a corporation may have major tax and legal consequences—before taking that step, be sure to consult with a tax professional and an attorney. For more information, see the *Family Child Care Legal and Insurance Guide.*

• •

Traditional Deductible IRA

The **traditional deductible IRA** is also referred to as a "regular" IRA. Your eligibility for this plan may depend on whether you or your spouse is "covered" by an employer's retirement plan. Bear in mind that if you or your spouse is eligible to participate in an employer-sponsored pension or IRA plan—either a 401(k) plan or a 403(b) plan—then you are "covered" by such a plan, even if that plan is optional, and you choose not to participate in it. (Remember that these plans offer the same tax advantages as an IRA.)

- **Eligibility**: The eligibility rules for this kind of IRA are as follows:

  - If you are single and not covered by an employer's retirement plan, then you are eligible to contribute to a regular IRA. (If you are single and covered by an employer's plan, talk to a tax professional to see if you are eligible to open this kind of IRA.)

  - If you are married, and neither you nor your spouse is covered by an employer's retirement plan, then you are eligible to contribute to a regular IRA.

  - If you are married, and either you or your spouse is covered by an employer's pension or retirement plan, then either of you may be eligible to contribute to a regular IRA, depending on your family income. For the current income requirements, ask the IRS, or talk to a tax professional.

- **Contribution limits**: You may contribute up to $5,000 to a regular IRA each year, and up to $6,000 each year if you are age 50 or older.

- **Deadlines**: You can set up and contribute to a regular IRA up to April 15 for the previous tax year, or up to October 15 if you file a tax extension. For example, if you wanted to claim a deduction for the 2008 tax year, you would have until April 15, 2009, to set up and contribute to your IRA account, and up to October 15, 2009, if you file an extension.

- **Tax deductibility and deferral**: Your contributions to a regular IRA are deductible up to the contribution limits each year. When you withdraw money from a regular IRA at retirement, you must pay income tax on both your contributions and your earnings on them.

- **Early withdrawal penalty**: There is a 10% penalty for withdrawing money from a regular IRA before age 59½. (However, there are exceptions for using the money for certain purposes, as described later in this chapter.)

Traditional Nondeductible IRA

A **traditional nondeductible IRA** is just what it sounds like. Although the contributions to this kind of IRA aren't tax deductible, it still offers you the benefit of deferring the tax on your contributions and earnings until you withdraw the money.

- **Eligibility**: Everyone is eligible to contribute to a nondeductible IRA; there are no income limits or rules about employer plan coverage.

- **Contribution limits and deadlines**: The maximum contributions and the deadlines for establishing and contributing to this kind of IRA are the same as for a regular IRA.

- **Tax deductibility and deferral**: The contributions to this kind of IRA aren't tax deductible, but this plan still allows you to defer the tax on your contributions and earnings until you withdraw the money.

- **Early withdrawal penalty**: There is a 10% penalty for withdrawing money from a nondeductible IRA before age 59½. There are a number of exceptions to this penalty, and they are somewhat different from those for other IRAs; for information, see IRS **Publication 590 Individual Retirement Arrangements**.

Roth IRA

The **Roth IRA** plan is named after Senator William Roth, one of the cosponsors of the law that created it. Your contributions to a Roth IRA aren't tax-deductible, as they are for other IRAs. However, a Roth IRA does offer a major benefit that other plans don't—your contributions and earnings are never taxed. A Roth IRA also offers more flexibility, since you don't have to start withdrawing your money when you reach age 70½—this means that you can pass on this money to your children or grandchildren, tax-free.

- **Eligibility**: The eligibility rules for a Roth IRA are as follows:

  - If you file as a single person or a head of household, you can contribute to a Roth IRA if your adjusted gross income (AGI) is less than $114,000.

  - If you are married and file jointly, you can contribute to a Roth IRA if your AGI is less than $166,000.

  - If you are married and file separately, you can contribute to a Roth IRA if your AGI is less than $10,000.

  Note: Contributions to a tax-deductible IRA will lower your adjusted gross income and thus make you more likely to qualify for a Roth IRA or claim other tax credits.

- **Contribution limits**: You may contribute up to $5,000 to a Roth IRA each year, and up to $6,000 each year if you are age 50 or older.

- **Deadlines**: You can set up and contribute to a Roth IRA up to April 15 for the previous tax year, or up to October 15 if you file a tax extension.

- **Tax deductibility and deferral**: Contributions to a Roth IRA are not tax-deductible as they are for a regular IRA. However, a Roth IRA is different from all other IRAs in that you never have to pay any income tax on your contributions or earnings as long as you withdraw your money after age 59½.

  In addition, you can withdraw your contributions from a Roth IRA before you reach age 59½ without paying an early withdrawal penalty. This gives you more flexibility in managing your money in case you need it before you reach age 59½.

- **Early withdrawal penalty**: If you withdraw your earnings from a Roth IRA before age 59½, you will have to pay a 10% penalty. However, there are several exceptions to this rule, including if you are disabled or if you are buying your first home.

SIMPLE IRA

The name of the **SIMPLE IRA** plan stands for "Savings Incentive Match Plan for Employees of Small Employers." As a self-employed person, for the purposes of this plan you're considered to be your own employee, which means that you can set up this kind of IRA for yourself. However, if you do that and have any employees, you may be required to set up and contribute to a SIMPLE IRA for your employees as well (according to the special rules listed below).

When you establish a SIMPLE IRA for an employee, you can either choose the fund for the employee (perhaps the same fund as your own SIMPLE IRA), or you can allow your employee to choose a fund. Once you set up a SIMPLE IRA for an employee, she can then decide to transfer her money to another investment, if she wishes.

Because the rules for establishing a SIMPLE IRA are more complicated than the rules for a regular or a Roth IRA, if you want to set up one of these plans, I recommend that you consult with a professional who is knowledgeable about IRAs.

- **Eligibility**: There are no income eligibility requirements for a SIMPLE IRA; any small employer or self-employed person can establish this kind of IRA.

- **Contribution limits**: As of 2008, you may contribute up to $10,500 of your business profit to your own SIMPLE IRA each year, and up to $13,000 if you are age 50 or older. The contributions that you make to your own SIMPLE IRA actually consist of two parts—an employee salary reduction and an employer match.

    When you contribute to your own SIMPLE IRA, you need to follow the special rules for employees (see below) to determine the amounts you can contribute in salary reduction and employer match. Be sure to keep records of how much you have contributed for each of these portions. Also note that these two portions have different deadlines (see below).

- **Deadlines**: Unlike other kinds of IRAs, you must establish a SIMPLE IRA at least 90 days before the end of the calendar year. The deadline for the employee salary reduction portion is January 31 of the next year. The deadline for the employer match portion is April 15 of the next year, or up to October 15 if you file a tax extension. (The same deadlines apply to contributions to an employee's SIMPLE IRA.)

- **Tax deductibility and deferral**: In a SIMPLE IRA that you set up for yourself, your contributions and earnings are both tax-deductible and subject to income tax when you withdraw them. You can also deduct as a business expense any contributions that you make to an employee's SIMPLE IRA plan each year. Your employee may deduct her own contributions to the plan each year, and when she withdraws money from the plan in retirement, she will need to pay taxes on both her earnings and the contributions that you both made to the plan.

- **Early withdrawal penalty**: The penalty for early withdrawal from a SIMPLE IRA is different from the rules for other kinds of IRAs—there's a 25% penalty for withdrawing money from a SIMPLE IRA in the first two years.

- **Special rules for employees**: There are some special rules that apply *if* you set up a SIMPLE IRA for yourself *and* you have any employees (either now or at any time in the future).

    If you open a SIMPLE IRA for yourself and you have one or more employees (or you hire someone to work for you at any time after you set up your plan), then you will be required to set up and contribute to a SIMPLE IRA for an employee if

  - she has earned at least $5,000 in any of the two preceding years; and
  - she can be reasonably expected to earn at least $5,000 in the current tax year.

You can also choose to set up a SIMPLE IRA for an employee even if she hasn't met the above criteria. In other words, you can set up a SIMPLE IRA for an employee who has earned less than $5,000 a year. However, if you set up a SIMPLE IRA for one employee, you'll have to allow all your employees who meet the above criteria to participate in the plan (by setting up and contributing to SIMPLE IRAs for them, unless they opt out).

Once you set up a SIMPLE IRA for an employee, then every year that she meets the above criteria you must contribute to her plan using one of the following formulas:

- You can match the employee's contribution to the plan, up to 3% of her salary; or
- you can contribute 2% of the employee's salary. In this case, the employee doesn't need to make any contributions to the plan.

You can use either formula, as long as you use the same method to contribute to the SIMPLE IRAs for all your employees. (You can switch formulas in any given year.) For example, let's say that your employee earns $12,000 per year:

- If you choose the 3% match option and your employee chips in the maximum amount of the employer match, $360 ($12,000 x 3% = $360), then you will have to match that by also contributing $360 to her SIMPLE IRA.

- If you choose the 2% option, you will be required to contribute $240 ($12,000 x 2% = $240), regardless of whether your employee has made any contributions to her plan.

Note that your contributions to the employee's plan are over and above the salary you pay her, not a payroll deduction. If one of your employees wants to make a monthly contribution to a SIMPLE IRA you have set up for her, then you will need to withhold the amount she has requested from her paycheck and deposit it on a monthly basis into her SIMPLE IRA. However, you can still wait until the April 15 deadline to make your contributions to her plan as her employer.

SEP IRA

The name of the **SEP IRA** plan stands for "Simplified Employee Pension." This IRA is similar to a SIMPLE IRA, in that you can set up a SEP IRA for yourself, as your own employee. However, if you have (another) employee, you may also have to set up and contribute to a plan for her. As a rule, a SIMPLE IRA is a better option than a SEP IRA, since a SIMPLE IRA will allow you to contribute more to your own plan.

- **Eligibility**: There are no income eligibility requirements for a SEP IRA; any small employer or self-employed person can establish this kind of IRA.

- **Contribution limits**: You may contribute up to 18.58% of your business profit (or a maximum contribution of $44,000) to a SEP IRA for yourself each year. For example, if your profit were $10,000, your maximum contribution to a SEP IRA would be $1,858.

- **Deadlines**: You can set up and contribute to a SEP IRA up to April 15 for the previous tax year, or up to October 15 if you file a tax extension.

- **Tax deductibility and deferral**: In a SEP IRA that you set up for yourself, your contributions and earnings are both tax-deductible and subject to income tax when they are withdrawn. You can also deduct as a business expense any contributions that you make to an employee's SEP IRA plan each year. Your employee may deduct her own contributions to the plan each year, and when she withdraws money from the plan in retirement, she'll need to pay taxes on both her earnings and the contributions that you both made to the plan.

- **Early withdrawal penalty**: There is a 10% penalty for withdrawing money from a SEP IRA before age 59½.

- **Special rules for employees**: As for a SIMPLE IRA, there are special rules that apply *if* you have set up a SEP IRA for yourself *and* you have any employees. You must set up a SEP IRA for an employee and contribute to her plan if she

  - is at least age 21;
  - has worked for you in three of the past five years; and
  - has earned at least $500 in the current year.

If you have an employee who meets those criteria, you must contribute to her SEP IRA in the same ratio that you contribute to your own SEP IRA that year. For example, let's say that you made a business profit of $10,000, and you paid your employee $7,000. If that year you contributed 10% of your profit to your SEP IRA ($1,000), you would have to contribute 10% of your employee's salary ($700) to her SEP IRA.

As for a SIMPLE IRA, you also have the option of setting up a SEP IRA for an employee who doesn't meet the above criteria. For example, you could decide to establish a SEP IRA for an employee who was younger than 21 and had worked for you for less than a year.

• •

Warning: You Must Keep the IRS Updated!

If you set up a SEP IRA or SIMPLE IRA, either for yourself or for an employee, you may be required to update your plan with the IRS periodically. If you fail to do this, you may lose the ability to deduct your contributions from your tax return. Ask the investment company that is responsible for keeping the IRS updated. To make certain you are in compliance, you may want to consult with a financial advisor or tax professional who is knowledgeable about IRAs.

• •

Self-Employed 401(k) Plan

The **self-employed 401(k) plan** is a relatively new option. Although I'm treating this as another kind of IRA for the sake of simplicity, technically this is not an individual IRA but an employer-sponsored plan. (Since you are self-employed, you qualify as both employer and employee for the purposes of this plan.) Bear in mind that it's only advisable to open this kind of plan if you have at least $20,000 to contribute.

- **Eligibility**: There are no income requirements for a self-employed 401(k) plan. The only eligibility requirement is that you not have any employees (other than yourself), with one exception—you're still eligible for this plan if your only employee is your spouse.

- **Contribution limits**: The maximum you can contribute to a self-employed 401(k) plan each year is far larger than for other kinds of IRAs. Since the contribution limits are quite complex, if you're considering this option, you should consult with a professional who is knowledgeable about IRAs.

- **Deadlines**: You must set up a self-employed 401(k) plan by December 31, and by that deadline you must also decide how much you will contribute for that year and report it to the IRS. However, the deadline for actually making your contribution is April 15 of the following year, or October 15 if you file a tax extension.

- **Tax deductibility and deferral**: Your contributions are tax-deductible. When you withdraw money from a self-employed 401(k) plan, you must pay income tax on both your contributions and your earnings.

- **Early withdrawal penalty**: The penalty for early withdrawals from this plan follows the same rules as for a traditional deductible IRA.

- **Special rules**: Setting up a self-employed 401(k) plan is more complicated than for any other kind of IRA—there is even a provision that allows you to treat some of your contributions like a Roth IRA. To set up this kind of plan, you must choose a mutual fund company or retirement plan provider that offers this plan (some don't). Those that offer this kind of plan include Fidelity (www.fidelity.com; 800-544-5373) and T. Rowe Price (www.troweprice.com; 800-225-5132).

To set up a self-employed 401(k) plan, you will have to fill out an application form provided by the mutual fund company. A self-employed 401(k) plan will be subject to fees and tax reporting requirements that aren't required for other IRA plans. There are also additional reporting requirements if you have more than $250,000 in this plan.

• •

Other Kinds of Retirement Plans

In addition to the plans discussed above, there are some other kinds of tax-deductible retirement plans—such as Keogh plans and defined benefit plans—that I haven't discussed here because they are more complicated to set up. However, you shouldn't be considering those other kinds of plans unless you have tens of thousands of dollars to invest each year. To find out more about these other options, consult a financial advisor who is knowledgeable about IRAs.

• •

Additional Rules for IRAs

Table 14 summarizes the primary differences between the rules for the various IRA plans. Here are some additional rules to bear in mind in weighing the various plans:

* Once you set up an IRA for yourself, you don't have to make the same contribution again each year. In fact, you don't have to contribute to it every year—or ever again. However, since the purpose of setting up an IRA is to maximize your retirement savings, you will want to try to contribute something to the plan every year, or whenever possible.

* You can't contribute more than a total of $5,000 (or $6,000 if you are age 50 or older) to any combination of a traditional IRA, nondeductible IRA, or Roth IRA in the same tax year. For example, you could contribute $2,000 to a traditional IRA and another $3,000 to a Roth IRA in one year—but once you do that, you won't be able to make any more contributions to a nondeductible IRA. If you contribute more than these limits, you will have to pay a penalty. If you have any extra money to contribute, you could set up a new account to invest in the same fund outside of an IRA.

* You may be allowed to make withdrawals from an IRA before age 59½ without paying the usual early withdrawal penalty if you'll be using the money for certain exceptions, which include a down payment on a first home, major medical expenses, and certain kinds of higher education expenses (Roth only). Early withdrawals are also allowed if you become disabled or die (in which case your heirs will be making the withdrawal). If you're considering an early withdrawal, check with a tax professional or the IRS first to make sure that your withdrawal will qualify for an exception.

Table 14. Summary of IRA plans*

	Eligibility limits?	Maximum contribution (< age 50)	Contributions are deductible?	Contributions are taxed at withdrawal?	Earnings are taxed at withdrawal?	Deadline to establish	Deadline to contribute	Special rules for employees?
Traditional IRA	Yes	$5,000	Yes	Yes	Yes	April 15	April 15	No
Traditional nondeductible IRA	No	$5,000	No	Yes	Yes	April 15	April 15	No
Roth IRA	Yes	$5,000	No	No	No	April 15	April 15	No
SIMPLE IRA	No	$10,500 of profit	Yes	Yes	Yes	October 1 of plan year	April 15	Yes
SEP IRA	No	18.58% of profit	Yes	Yes	Yes	April 15	April 15	Yes
Self-employed 401(k) plan	No	$45,000	Yes	Yes	Yes	December 31	April 15	No

*This table simplifies certain plan rules for comparison purposes; for more information, refer to the full description of each plan in this chapter.

Note: The above information is subject to change, especially the amount that you are allowed to contribute each year. Check the current requirements before you establish your IRA.

- You can't contribute to your own SIMPLE IRA and SEP IRA in the same year. You can contribute to one of these plans in one year and then to the other plan in the next year. (If you have set up these plans for your employees, the special rules for employees will determine whether you'll have to contribute to an employee's plan in any given year.)

- You aren't allowed to establish both a SIMPLE IRA and a self-employed 401(k) plan for your business.

- You can contribute to a Roth IRA, SIMPLE IRA, or SEP IRA yourself even if your spouse is contributing to a 401(k) plan offered by his employer.

- Your contributions to an IRA or a self-employed 401(k) plan won't reduce the Social Security taxes that you must pay on your business profit each year. However, any contributions that you make to an employee's IRA will reduce your Social Security taxes.

Bear in mind that these rules may change from year to year—especially the maximum contribution limits. Therefore, before you choose an IRA, you should get the latest information by consulting a tax advisor or IRS **Publication 590 Individual Retirement Arrangements**.

Choosing Between the IRA Plans

With all of the choices that are available, how can you decide which IRA is best for you? Here are some guidelines that can help you decide.

If you are looking for an immediate tax benefit for your IRA contributions, that will limit your choices to a traditional IRA, SIMPLE IRA, SEP IRA, or self-employed 401(k) plan. However, bear in mind that all of these choices will require you to pay taxes on your money when you withdraw it. Therefore, you'll want to consider the tax bracket you expect to be in when you withdraw the money. Since the tax issues involved in this choice can be complicated, I recommend that you consult a tax professional in this case.

The traditional nondeductible IRA doesn't have the advantage of either tax deductibility or the benefit of avoiding taxes on your earnings like the Roth IRA. So when would you consider a traditional nondeductible IRA? There are two scenarios in which you might consider this option:

- You aren't eligible for either a Roth IRA or a traditional IRA.

- You are now in a low tax bracket, but you expect to be in a much higher tax bracket after retirement.

However, even in this case, it may make more sense to open a SIMPLE IRA or a SEP IRA rather than a traditional nondeductible IRA, as long as you either can rule out the possibility that you will ever hire an employee or wouldn't mind contributing to an employee's retirement plan.

Next we'll look more closely at the factors to weigh while choosing between a SIMPLE and a SEP IRA or a traditional and a Roth IRA. I'll also explain how to choose an employee IRA for your spouse or child.

A SIMPLE IRA or a SEP IRA?

If you have (now or in the future) any employees, a SIMPLE IRA and a SEP IRA have the same tax advantages and similar drawbacks. You should pause before opening either of these IRAs if you have an employee now or might conceivably hire someone to help you in the future. Otherwise, you could end up being required to set up and contribute to an IRA for your employee.

If you're sure that you won't ever be hiring any employees, then a SIMPLE IRA is a better choice than the SEP IRA, since a SIMPLE IRA will allow you to contribute more money toward your retirement. Here's an example: if your business profit were $10,000, the maximum you could contribute to a SEP IRA would be $1,858 (18.58% of your profit). However, you'd be able to contribute the full $10,000 that you made to a SIMPLE IRA, since the maximum contribution limit is $10,500 of your profit.

If you can only afford to contribute $1,000 to an IRA this year, then it doesn't matter which of these two IRAs you set up. Just bear in mind that a SIMPLE IRA will give you more flexibility to make larger contributions in later years. Since this is the only difference between these two IRA plans if you don't have employees, a SIMPLE IRA has the advantage over a SEP IRA.

A Roth IRA or a Traditional IRA?

If you really need the tax deduction now, then a traditional IRA may be a better choice than a Roth IRA. However, if you can wait until retirement to get your tax savings, then a Roth IRA may be a better choice. A Roth IRA is also more flexible, since you don't have to start withdrawing money once you reach age 70½, which will allow you to pass on your money to your children or grandchildren tax-free. The longer you have until retirement, the greater advantage a Roth IRA will have over a traditional IRA.

Choosing between a Roth IRA and traditional IRA can be a complex decision, and there are many factors that may influence your choice, including your age, tax bracket, retirement investments, and the amount of money that you want to leave to your heirs. So this may not be simply a financial decision. For help with this choice, I suggest that you consult a financial advisor who is knowledgeable about IRAs.

Converting a Regular IRA to a Roth IRA

If you have a regular IRA and have decided that a Roth IRA would meet your needs better, you can roll over the money in your regular IRA into a new Roth IRA. To be eligible for a Roth conversion, your adjusted gross income (the bottom line on your **Form 1040**) must be below certain limits set by Congress. I won't describe the limits here, since they are complex and likely to change, but they are relatively high, and most providers should qualify. (For the latest limits, ask your tax preparer, or see IRS **Publication 590 Individual Retirement Arrangements**.) There are no minimum or maximum limits on the amount that you may convert to a Roth IRA.

However, there may be a significant cost involved in this kind of conversion. If you are converting contributions that you have already deducted on your tax return, then you will have to pay income taxes on all the money that you earned in your regular IRA. Furthermore, if you want to use money from your regular IRA to pay these taxes, this will be considered an early withdrawal from the plan and will be subject to the 10% penalty. Therefore, it's best to pay these taxes out of your pocket, if possible.

If you do have to pay the taxes from the IRA funds you are converting, then the tax benefits of converting the money will be greatly diminished, and you may want to reconsider this option. Also, bear in mind that declaring this income now may put you into a higher tax bracket, thus disqualifying you from other tax benefits this year, such as the Earned Income Credit or the Saver's Credit.

The good news is that you won't have to pay the usual 10% early withdrawal penalty on the conversion itself—just on any funds that you withdraw while converting the account. Since a Roth conversion is not a simple decision, if you are considering this option, I suggest that you consult a financial advisor who is knowledgeable about IRAs.

• •

Other IRA Conversions

There are other IRA conversions that you might want to consider:

- You can convert the money from an employer plan directly into a Roth IRA. This is typically done when you leave the employer. However, if your employer's plan allows, you may be able to do this kind of conversion while you are still participating in the plan.

- You can convert funds from a SIMPLE IRA to a Roth IRA, as long as you have participated in the SIMPLE IRA for at least two years.

• •

Setting up an IRA for a Spouse or Child

If you hire your spouse or child to work in your business, you may want to establish an IRA to provide tax benefits for that family member's own retirement plan. Although you can set up this account as a SIMPLE IRA or a SEP IRA, there will be less paperwork involved if you set it up as a traditional or Roth IRA.

Here's an example of how this would work. Let's assume that you pay your daughter Magdalena $4,000 a year to work in your business, and you want to contribute some or all of that $4,000 into an IRA for her retirement.

One option would be to set up a traditional IRA for Magdalena. If she earns less than $5,350 in wages (2007 limit), she won't have to pay any federal income taxes, and therefore she won't get a tax deduction for her IRA contributions. However, she'll still be able to defer paying taxes on her earnings over the years.

A second, and perhaps better, option would be to set up a Roth IRA for Magdalena. This would allow her to withdraw money for her retirement without ever paying taxes on her contributions or on the earnings from her investment. This may be the best choice for a child, since the advantages of a Roth IRA over a traditional IRA will accumulate over time.

Under either of these options (Roth IRA or regular IRA), Magdalena would be able to withdraw money from her account before she reaches age 59½ without a penalty under certain conditions. She could use the money to pay for a down payment on her first home or (with the Roth IRA) her higher education expenses.

If you establish a SIMPLE IRA or a SEP IRA for yourself, and then hire your spouse or child, you may be required to set up and contribute to the family member's IRA, as outlined in the special rules for employees under each plan. If you hire your spouse to work in your business, and he is eligible for a Roth IRA, then he will be able to make contributions to his own Roth IRA. For information about other tax rules for hiring members of your family, see the latest edition of the *Family Child Care Tax Workbook and Organizer*.

Tax Credit for Low-Income Taxpayers

If your family has a low income, you may be eligible to claim the federal Saver's Credit for your IRA contributions. This can make a big difference in your income taxes, since tax credits reduce the taxes that you owe dollar for dollar—unlike tax deductions, which simply reduce the income on which your taxes are based. If you qualify for this tax credit, you can add these savings to your savings from deducting your IRA contributions, making an IRA an even better deal for you.

The eligibility limits for this credit are likely to change every year or two. However, to give you a rough idea of whether you might qualify, to be eligible for this credit in the 2008 tax year, your adjusted gross income had to be

- $53,000 or less if you were married and filing jointly
- $39,750 or less if you were a head of household
- $26,500 or less if you were a single taxpayer or married and filing separately

To claim this credit, you must be over 18 years old, and you can't be a full-time student or a dependent on another taxpayer's return. If you otherwise qualify but your income isn't under the limits shown above, be sure to check the current limits.

You can apply this tax credit to the contributions you make to any of the six kinds of IRAs described in this chapter, as well as to any contributions that you or your spouse may make to an employer-sponsored 401(k) or 403(b) retirement plan. The maximum annual contribution that is eligible for this credit is $2,000 per person. The amount of your tax credit will range from 10% to 50% of your total contribution, depending on your income.

If you haven't been making regular contributions to your retirement fund because you didn't think you could afford it, this tax credit can give you a big incentive to increase your contributions.

For example, let's say that you're married, and you and your spouse file your 2008 taxes jointly, showing an adjusted gross income of $29,000. Since your income is below the 2008 limit, you're eligible to claim the Saver's Credit that year. If you contributed $1,000 to a SIMPLE IRA that year, you would receive a $500 tax credit for that contribution. In addition, if you're in the 15% tax bracket, your tax deduction for that contribution would save you about $150 in taxes. This adds up to a tax savings of about $650. (If you made contributions to a Roth IRA instead, you'd still get the $500 tax credit, but not the $150 tax savings, since contributions to a Roth IRA aren't tax-deductible.)

In this example, it only cost you about $350 to add $1,000 to your retirement fund! Because of the tremendous benefits of this credit, I strongly recommend that you check if you qualify for it each year—and if you do, take advantage of it. To claim the Saver's Credit, fill out **Form 8880** and then report the amount of your credit on **Form 1040** (on the line that says "Retirement savings contributions credit").

If you qualified for this tax credit and contributed to an IRA in a previous tax year, but didn't claim this credit, you can use **Form 1040X** to file an amended return and get a refund, as long as you do so within three years. (For more information about filing an amended return, see the latest edition of the *Tax Workbook and Organizer*.)

Note: Some providers hire their own children to work in their business and set up an IRA in each child's name. If you do this, bear in mind that your contributions to this IRA won't qualify for this tax credit if the child is your dependent, too young, or a full-time student.

Prioritize Your Retirement Investments

It can be quite challenging to figure out which kind of IRA plan to set up first. Yet it's difficult to provide any simple guidelines in this area, since the best plan will depend on your individual circumstances. (If your choice doesn't seem clear, you may want to consult a financial advisor or do more research before making a decision.)

However, it's important to pick a plan and try to get started as soon as possible—you can always move your money into another kind of IRA later. So despite my warning, I'm going to offer some guidelines for prioritizing your retirement plans after all. Just be sure to weigh these suggestions in the context of your individual circumstances.

1. If you're married and your spouse's employer matches contributions to its 401(k) or 403(b) retirement plan, then your first priority should be contributing enough money to get the full employer match for that plan. For example, if your spouse makes $35,000 a year and his employer contributes up to 2% of his salary, this means that his employer will match the first $700 a year ($35,000 x 2% = $700) that your spouse contributes.

   This extra $700 is free money that you should always aim for first, even if the investment choices in the employer's plan aren't the best. You can always move the money to another investment later, or after your spouse leaves the job.

   If you're single and not covered by an employer plan, see step 2 below.

2. The next decision will be deciding whether to contribute more money to your spouse's retirement plan or to open a Roth IRA. For most family child care providers, the best approach would be to open a Roth IRA, if you qualify. Bear in mind that you can invest in two or more funds for your Roth IRA—for example, you could open a stock fund and a bond fund and designate them both as Roth IRAs. However, no matter how many different Roth IRA accounts you have, your total contributions each year can't exceed the annual limit. So if you are younger than age 50, the cumulative total that you can contribute to all your Roth IRAs each year is $5,000.

    If you're single and not covered by an employer plan, then a Roth IRA will be your first investment priority.

3. Once you're contributing the maximum amount to Roth IRAs for both you and your spouse (either $10,000 or $12,000 per year for the two of you), the next decision will be whether to contribute more money to your spouse's retirement plan or to establish a SIMPLE IRA.

    If your spouse's 401(k) plan has good investment choices, then it may not make any difference whether you increase your contributions to that plan or open a SIMPLE IRA, since the tax advantages will be the same. However, if the choices in the employer's plan are poor—for example, if they are heavily weighted toward the company's stock—then it will make more sense to put your money into a SIMPLE IRA. (To learn how to evaluate the fund options in your spouse's employer retirement plan, see chapter 15.)

    If you're single, I'd suggest that you open a SIMPLE IRA after fully funding your Roth IRA.

4. If you have fully funded your spouse's employer plan, a Roth IRA, and a SIMPLE IRA, and you have at least $20,000 in additional funds to invest for retirement, then consider opening a self-employed 401(k) plan. If you have less than that, put the money into a taxable non-IRA retirement account. If the account eventually grows to $20,000, then withdraw it, and use it to open a self-employed 401(k) plan.

How to Set Up an IRA

Once you have decided to set up an IRA, how do you get started? Setting up an IRA requires two decisions: *(a)* choosing an investment—such as stocks, bonds, or real estate; and then *(b)* choosing the kind of IRA that will provide the best tax benefits for your circumstances.

You can set up just about any investment as an IRA. As described in the previous chapter, when you open an investment in a mutual fund, simply tell the company that you want that investment to be an IRA, and they will explain what paperwork you'll need to fill out. You may also be able to set up an IRA through your bank or credit union, and you can also set up IRAs through a stock broker or a financial advisor.

Don't forget to set up all your retirement investments as IRAs—the tax advantages are significant and will make a real difference in the amount of money that you'll end up with after you retire.

CHAPTER SEVENTEEN

Working with a Financial Advisor

Chapter Summary

This chapter describes how to find, interview, and select a financial advisor. It also explains how to update your plan with your advisor every year and how to evaluate whether your advisor is doing a good job for you.

After having read this far, you may feel confident in your ability to make your own retirement planning decisions and manage your own investments. Or you may still be hesitant to trust your own judgment in this new area, despite understanding the importance of starting promptly.

Maybe you're not that interested in trying to master this subject and would like some guidance. Or perhaps you're faced with a complex financial issue that you know you won't be able to sort through by yourself. You may have asked for help from more experienced child care providers and still not be sure how to proceed. For any of these reasons, at some point you may decide that you need professional assistance with your financial issues.

Getting help with your retirement planning is a very good reason to consult a financial advisor, since the plans you make now will determine the options that will be available to you after retirement. A qualified advisor can also help you sort through the ins and outs of various kinds of IRAs and decide which one is best for your circumstances.

Professional advice may also be useful if you're experiencing a life transition that has major financial consequences—such as a marriage, a divorce, the birth or adoption of a child, the purchase of a home, or a change in your spouse's work status—or if you've experienced a sudden change in your financial situation, such as an inheritance. You might also want to consult a financial advisor if you're grappling with a financial need that isn't discussed in this book, such as saving for college, planning your estate, or drafting a will.

In all of these cases, a professional advisor can give you a better understanding of your options and guide you in choosing among them.

Finding a Financial Advisor

Some people hesitate to hire a financial advisor because they're afraid to trust someone else with their money. As one provider commented, "I don't know where to go to set up a financial retirement account. I worry that a financial advisor will take advantage of me or give me bad advice."

You can reduce the chances that you will choose the wrong person by following certain guidelines for finding and choosing an advisor. First, locate the advisors in your area who have the proper professional credentials and are qualified to provide the kind of help you need. Then interview each of them, and choose the one who seems to be the best match for you, as described below.

Start by asking around to see if you can gather some names of good financial advisors. In addition to your friends and acquaintances, you might ask for recommendations from professionals such as your tax preparer, business liability insurance agent, or lawyer. The best recommendations are likely to come from people you respect, who share your values and emotional attitudes about money, and who have successfully resolved issues similar to those you are grappling with.

Financial Planning Credentials

Anyone can set up shop as a "financial advisor" or "financial planner"—there are no regulations about who can use these titles. Unfortunately, some of the people who call themselves "financial advisors" are really just trying to sell you a financial product. An advisor who is only interested in pushing you to buy something won't have your best interests in mind.

To help rule out these kinds of advisors, it's important to limit your search to people who have earned a professional credential based on formal standards of practice and a code of ethics. However, just because a person has one of these credentials doesn't mean that the person is qualified to advise you. You'll still need to interview the person and evaluate whether she'll be a good match for you, as I'll explain below.

The best-known and most basic credential for providing financial advice is **certified financial planner** (CFP). There are about 50,000 CFPs across the country. To get this credential, a person must pass six national licensing exams, take a two-day test, and have at least three years' experience working with clients.

Once certified, a person who has this credential is qualified to provide advice about retirement planning, investments, taxes, estate, and insurance. To learn more about the CFP credential, or to find a CFP in your area, visit www.cfp.net, or call the Institute of Certified Financial Planners at 800-282-7526.

In researching financial advisors, you may also see many other kinds of initials listed after a person's name, including CPA, PFS, EA, RIA, and ChFC. Here's a short guide to what each of these professional credentials means:

- A CPA is a **certified public accountant**; this credential qualifies a person to do accounting for a business, but it doesn't qualify her to offer financial advice to individuals. However, a CPA who has at least five years of financial planning experience can apply to be accredited as a **personal financial specialist** (PFS). To learn more about the PFS credential, visit the Web site of the American Institute of Certified Public Accountants, www.aicpa.org. To find a CPA near you, visit www.cpadirectory.com, or call 800-CPA-DIRECT.

- An EA is an **enrolled agent**. This credential means that the person has passed a two-day IRS test and is certified to represent clients in an IRS tax audit. (Some EAs are also CFPs.) Many EAs also offer financial planning services; usually they start by doing taxes and then move on to financial planning. For more information about EAs, contact the National Association of Enrolled Agents at www.naea.org or 202-822-6232.

  Note: There can be an advantage in having your tax preparer act as your financial advisor. Finding one person who understands both your financial decisions and their tax implications may be easier, and less expensive, than hiring both a financial planner and a tax preparer.

- An RIA is a **registered investment advisor**. This credential means the person is registered with the state and is in the business of providing investment advice. To find an RIA go to www.investmentadvisorsearch.com.

- A ChFC is a **chartered financial consultant**. This credential focuses on providing advice about insurance needs, investments, and taxes. These advisors usually start as life insurance agents and then move into financial planning. For more information go to www.investorwords.com/834/Chartered_Financial_Consultant.html.

• •

Does Your Investment Company Offer Advice?

The large mutual fund companies such as Fidelity, Schwab, and Vanguard are another potential source of financial planning help. Many of these companies offer retirement planning and investment counseling for their clients, or potential clients, at a low cost or free of charge. Table 12 (in chapter 15) provides the contact information for four major mutual fund companies.

• •

Although it's important to find a person who is qualified to provide financial advice, also bear in mind that just because someone has one of the credentials listed above or is a member of a solid professional organization doesn't necessarily mean that she would be a good advisor for you. For example, some financial advisors only want to work with people who have a lot of money to invest—these professionals generally charge very high fees, so their services probably won't be affordable.

One way to find a financial advisor whom you *can* afford is to search through a network of financial professionals who are paid on an hourly, as needed, basis. Two such networks are the Garrett Planning Network (www.garrettplanningnetwork.com; 866-260-8400) and the National Association of Personal Financial Advisors (www.napfa.org; 800-333-6659).

What Kind of Help Do You Need?

In choosing a financial advisor, it will be helpful to think about what kind of help you're looking for. Do you need advice about where to invest your money? Are you trying to choose an IRA? Are you just looking for more general assistance with managing your finances?

If you aren't sure what you really need, look for someone who's knowledgeable about a broad range of financial issues, such as retirement planning, estate planning, budgeting, reducing debt, college funding, and selling a home. Such an advisor can look at your financial situation from a broad perspective and explain the best way to move forward.

Choosing a Financial Advisor

Once you have gathered some referrals to qualified financial advisors, contact each one, and set up an in-person interview. (You shouldn't have to pay a potential financial advisor for the time needed for this interview.)

There are several questions that you should ask in the interview to see if the advisor is a good match for you. However, the two most important areas to consider are topics that the advisor should bring up with you—she should ask you about your risk tolerance, and she should clearly explain how she'll be paid for her services. Although you shouldn't have to initiate these topics, be sure to ask enough questions so that you can decide if you feel comfortable with this advisor's approach.

Risk Tolerance

In your interview, the financial advisor should make it a priority to ask about your tolerance for investment risk. In response, be very clear about your comfort level with risk. Some people lose sleep whenever the stock market dips a bit; others are looking for ways to "beat the market." No matter how you feel about risk, you need to feel confident that your financial planner understands and respects your position. (Whenever your advisor advises you to make an investment, be sure to ask her about the risks associated with that investment.)

Payment Method

In your interview, the financial advisor should clearly explain how she'll be paid. The most common payment methods are fee-only, commission-only, or a combination of the two.

- A fee-only planner is paid (by you) for providing advice; she receives no commissions on any products she advises you to buy.

- A commission-only planner provides "free" advice but gets a commission (from a third party) whenever she sells you a financial product.

There's no simple rule about which of these payment methods is best—there are good financial advisors who use each of these methods. In the long run, an advisor's competence and ethical standards are far more important than the way she is compensated. However, you do need to understand how each advisor you interview is paid and decide if you feel comfortable with that method.

• •

Warning Signs

Here are some potential warning signs to note when interviewing a potential financial advisor:

- Never hire a financial advisor who asks you to hand over complete control of your money. The final decisions should always be up to you.

- Ask to see some of the financial plans the advisor has prepared for her other clients. Are the plans difficult for you to understand? Does the advisor seem to be giving the same advice to all her clients? If the answer to either of these questions is yes, it's a bad sign.

- If a planner promises to beat the stock market average, be wary! This may mean that she'll be taking more risks with your money than you'd like.

• •

Find a Good Match

Here are some areas that you should ask about in the interview to see if you and the financial advisor are a good match for each other:

- Ask about the advisor's investment philosophy. You should feel comfortable with her approach to investing.

- Ask the advisor about her typical client profile—for example, is she used to working with retirees, middle-income people, and business clients? Her typical client should fall roughly in your income range—if your income is well below her average, your concerns may not have her full attention. If your income is well above her average, she may not have the expertise to advise you properly.

- Ask to see the returns that the advisor's plans have produced over the last several years. However, bear in mind that any financial planner with 10 or more years' experience will have been through ups and downs in the stock market. Don't expect her returns to be above average every year.

- Ideally, you're looking for a long-term relationship with your financial advisor. Ask her what will happen to your account if she moves away, leaves the business, or dies. Does she have a transition plan? Who will take over her clients?

Before you make a final choice:

- Ask for at least three references from clients who have worked with the advisor for at least five years.

- Get a written agreement that outlines the services you will receive and how much they will cost you.

In making your choice, bear in mind that a good financial advisor is someone who will listen to you and be a mentor or coach to help you make good decisions. Your advisor can help you diversify your investments and reallocate them as you grow older. She can also be helpful by encouraging you to stick with your long-term investment plan if you tend to react emotionally to the ups and downs of the stock market.

Too many people fail to reach their financial goals because they invest their money emotionally and move it around in response to every minor setback. It can be very useful to have someone you trust who can calm your anxieties and provide objective counsel before you make a change.

Working with Your Financial Advisor

One you hire a financial advisor and set up your investment plan, you should be in touch with her at least once a year. At this meeting, discuss with her any changes or events in your family that year such as a divorce, illness, birth, or the loss or change of a job. Review whether your risk tolerance has changed and whether you want to reevaluate your investment plan.

There are three questions that you should ask in your annual meeting:

- How well did my investments do? (What was my percent return on an annual basis?)

- After all fees are subtracted, how does the return on my investments compare with similar investments?

- What did your services cost me?

Is Your Advisor Doing a Good Job for You?

Since the stock market will go up and down over the years, there may be quarters, or even years, when your investments will lose money. That's the nature of investment risk, and it shouldn't worry you or your advisor. (For an explanation of investment risk, see chapter 14.) So how can you tell if your advisor is doing a good job for you? Here are some tips:

- Does your advisor return your phone calls and get back to you promptly? When you talk, does she provide clear, helpful answers to your questions?

- Are you getting quarterly financial reports that clearly describe how well your investments are doing? (If you see something that you don't understand on your quarterly statement, don't hesitate to call your advisor and ask what it means.)

- If you tend to get emotional about your investments, does your advisor remind you of your long-term goals and help you stay focused on your plan?

- Is your advisor able to clearly explain your investments to you and describe why each one is part of your portfolio? (If you don't recognize a fund that is listed on your quarterly statement, ask what that fund is, why you are invested in it, and how it fits your risk tolerance profile.)

- Does your advisor follow your preferences in taking on investment risk? (If you aren't sure, ask. If you can't get a clear answer, that's not a good sign.)

If your advisor is continuing to do a good job for you, the answers to all of these questions will be yes.

• •

It's Your Money

No matter how much you trust your financial advisor, you can't give up the responsibility for your own financial decisions. You may not always agree with your advisor's recommendations, and you need to know enough to understand what she's suggesting so that you can decide if it is right for you. Therefore, hiring someone to advise you doesn't mean that you can simply stop educating yourself about investing and managing your money.

When your advisor makes a recommendation, ask questions until you're sure that you understand the risks and benefits of the path she's proposing. Remember, it's your money, and you're the one who'll have to live with the results. So the final decision should always be up to you.

• •

It's Not Just about the Money

The goal of this book has been to help you keep, save, and invest the money that you're earning in a caring profession. I hope you have learned a few things about gaining more control over your money and will be able to make wiser investment decisions to help your money work harder for you in the future.

However, the truth is that for most providers a family child care business is not really about making money. In our survey, many providers clearly stated that money wasn't their top priority:

> *This is the lowest-paying job ever—I do it for the love of the children. If it wasn't for my husband's job, and the insurance his employer offers, I'd never be able to do this.*

> *I love what I do, and I'd take a pay cut any day to be at home when my children come home from school. No one can love your children as you do.*

> *Do child care for the love of it. You can stay home with your kids while they're small and get a little money to try to keep your family afloat. But also have a plan that will allow you to rejoin the workforce once your own little ones are in school.*

> *How many wage earners get as many hugs as we do every day?*

> *Caring for children is a special kind of investing in all of our futures.*

Although some family child care providers see this business as a short-term option while their own children are young, others expect the money they are earning to support them in a long-term career. There's plenty of room for you to make your own decisions about the importance of money in your business.

Some providers feel that it's useless to even try to approach this business from a money-making perspective because of the chronically low rates of pay in the child care field:

Leave this profession. It won't support your current or future financial viability.

Get back into the workforce, and get a job with benefits.

Don't become a child care provider.

You just can't survive on day care alone.

Unless the government finds some way to offer incentives to high-quality, well-educated providers, we just won't be able to continue doing this much longer.

It's true that some providers have failed to make a living in this field through no fault of their own—and many others who remain in this business are struggling to get by on a very low income. There are many nonfinancial reasons why you might choose to continue—and I salute all of you who work in this field, regardless of how much money you're making.

A 2007 study that reviewed the last 20 years of research on family child care found that most providers reported that they were satisfied with their work, citing advantages such as being self-employed, being able to stay home with their children, and not having to worry about the usual job requirements.[*]

In their excellent book *Your Money or Your Life*, Joe Dominguez and Vicki Robin write that "money is something we choose to trade our life energy for. Our life energy is our allotment of time here on earth, the hours of precious life available to us. When we go to our job we are trading our life energy for money." Sadly, many people in our society are working mainly to earn the money to buy more things. They work hard all their lives at a job that has little true meaning, hoping for the reward of a few years of retirement in which to finally enjoy their life.

Despite the financial limitations that some family child care providers experience, most of you say that you are finding a greater reward and purpose in serving children and making a positive contribution to our collective future. You feel good about your work because the hours of your "precious life" are being well spent.

Your love of children and the satisfaction that you get from watching them grow are experiences that can never be measured in money.

---

[*] Taryn W. Morrissey, "Family Child Care in the United States," Child Care & Early Education Research Connections (March 2007), www.researchconnections.org.

APPENDIX

Resources

Web Resources

This section lists all the Web sites mentioned in this book by chapter, with a brief explanation of the topic involved. For more information, see the chapter. (This list doesn't include the references to our Web sites, www.redleafpress.org and www.resourcesforchildcare.org.)

Chapter One

Living on less

www.thefrugalshopper.com

www.simpleliving.net

www.frugaliving.com

Value of used items

itsdeductibleonline.intuit.com

Chapter Two

Online savings accounts

www.ingdirect.com

www.emigrantdirect.com

www.gmacbank.com

Money market funds

www.franklintempleton.com

www.fidelity.com

www.aarpfinancial.com

www.tiaa-cref.org

CD rates

www.bankrate.com.

Short-term bond funds

www.fidelity.com

www.schwab.com

www.troweprice.com

www.vanguard.com

Survey about children and money

www.cbanet.org/SURVEYS/literacy/Report.pdf

Teaching children about money

www.moneyinstructor.com/kids.asp

www.extension.umn.edu/distribution/
youthdevelopment/DA6116.html

www.msgen.com

www.finance.yahoo.com/how-to-guide/
family-home/12820

Chapter Three

Credit rating companies

www.experian.com

www.equifax.com

www.transunion.com

Credit report orders

www.annualcreditreport.com

Compare current credit card interest rates

www.creditcards.com

www.bankrate.com

www.indexcreditcards.com

Paying down your debt

www.debtreductionservices.org

Credit counseling ("Financing Family Child Care")

www.enterprisecommunity.org/resources/
publications_catalog/#child

Chapter Four

No Web resources

Chapter Five

No Web resources

Chapter Six

Vehicle buying guide and reliability ratings

www.ConsumerReports.org

Used vehicle history

www.carfax.com

Chapter Seven

Loan resources for family child care

www.ncfn.org/ff.htm

www.ChildCareAware.org

nccic.acf.hhs.gov/poptopics/micro-directory.html

www.sba.gov

Chapter Seven (continued)

Getting a bank loan ("Financing Family Child Care")

> www.enterprisecommunity.org/resources/
> publications_catalog/#child

Chapter Eight

Employer identification number

> www.irs.gov

NAFCC Code of Ethical Conduct

> www.nafcc.org

Chapter Nine

No Web resources

Chapter Ten

Divorce resources

> www.womansdivorce.com

Social Security benefits after divorce

> www.socialsecurity.gov

Chapter Eleven

Social Security statement and retirement benefits

> www.socialsecurity.gov

Chapter Twelve

Retirement issues for women

> www.wiserwomen.org

Source of table 8 (online worksheet)

> www.choosetosave.org/ballpark

Online retirement calculators

> www.aarp.org
>
> www.fidelity.com
>
> www.smartmoney.com
>
> www.choosetosave.org
>
> www.cnnmoney.com
>
> www.hughchou.org

Chapter Thirteen

No Web resources

Chapter Fourteen

Online risk tolerance surveys

> moneycentral.msn.com—search for "Risk
> Tolerance Quiz"
>
> www.icief.org/risk/risk_quiz.html

Reverse mortgages

> www.aarp.org/money/revmort

"Personal Finance" in Sunday Wall Street Journal

> www.sunday.wsj.com

Magazines on investing and money management

> www.kiplinger.com
>
> www.smartmoney.com
>
> money.cnn.com—click on "Personal Finance"
> and then on "Money Magazine"

Retirement issues for women

> www.wiserwomen.org
>
> www.wife.org/money_retirement.htm

Investment clubs

> www.betterinvesting.org
>
> groups.google.com—search for discussion
> groups on investment clubs
>
> www.investopedia.com/articles/01/062001.asp

Cooperative extension offices

> www.csrees.usda.gov

Retirement planning and personal finance

> moneycentral.msn.com
>
> www.tiaa-cref.org
>
> www.financialengines.com
>
> www.retireonyourterms.org
>
> www.morningstar.com
>
> www.retireearlyhomepage.com
>
> www.kiplinger.com
>
> www.americasaves.org
>
> www.consumerreports.org

Chapter Fifteen

Pax World Balanced Fund

    www.paxworld.com

Third Avenue Value Fund

    www.thirdavenuefunds.com

Four major investment companies

    www.fidelity.com

    www.schwab.com

    www.troweprice.com

    www.vanguard.com

Companies that offer REITs

    www.vanguard.com

    www.wellsref.com

    www.amex.com

Annuities

    www.annuityfyi.com

    www.iii.org/individuals/annuities

    www.navanet.org

    www.sec.gov/investor/pubs/varannty.htm

Low initial investment

    www.tiaa-cref.org

    www.schwab.com

    www.paxworld.com

    www.morningstar.com

Chapter Sixteen

Self-employed 401(k) plans

    www.fidelity.com

    www.troweprice.com

Chapter Seventeen

Financial planning credentials

    www.cfp.net

    www.aicpa.org

    www.cpadirectory.com

    www.naea.org

Networks of financial planners

    www.garrettplanningnetwork.com

    www.napfa.org